CW01666267

CAN'T BREAK ME

16 Inspiring Women's Quest For
Success In The Face Of Adversity

Queens In Business

CAN'T BREAK ME
16 Inspiring Women's Quest For Success In The Face Of Adversity

ISBN: 978-1-7385347-0-8 Paperback

Published By: Inspired By Publishing

Cover Designed By: Tanya Grant - The TNG Designs Group Limited

Acknowledgements

By Chloë Bisson

Co-Founder of Queens In Business

Our resilience has roots in our childhood, and believe it or not, every step we took, resilient in its own way, has led us to this moment. I've navigated through life's toughest challenges and seemingly trivial hurdles, and in reflecting upon my own journey, resilience stands out as the biggest force propelling me to where I am today.

Gratitude is owed to three extraordinary women who played a crucial role in influencing the present—my fellow Co-Founders: Sunna Coleman, Shim Ravalia, and Tanya Grant. These inspiring entrepreneurs have shown that by staying devoted to one's purpose amid life's unexpected challenges, one can not only endure but genuinely blossom on the other side.

Within the pages of this book, you'll discover stories featuring sixteen female entrepreneurs who, fueled by resilience, discovered how setbacks could be transformed into the driving force behind their destinies, refusing to let adversity define them.

I'd like to say thank you to our dedicated publishing team members, Angela Haynes-Ranger and Gaby Osias whose talent for storytelling makes this book possible. To Tanya Grant, whose artistic touch consistently graces all of our book covers, and to Alex Padua for making sure all elements are prepared seamlessly for publication.

Finally, on behalf of all of us at Queens In Business, we thank you for allowing us to accompany you on your personal journey to resilience. We trust that these stories will serve as companions, offering encouragement, lessons, and reminders of how capable you truly are.

Dedication

This book is dedicated to every woman who has faced challenges with unyielding determination, whose resilience has transformed trials into triumphs and whose unwavering spirit has paved the way for others to soar.

With love,
Queens In Business Club

Table of Contents

Introduction

Through the golden thread that binds these chapters together, we experience triumph, adversity and transformation in ways we may never have imagined.

We embark on a compelling journey through the untold stories of 16 remarkable women who have defied the odds, overcome challenges, and emerged as beacons of inspiration in the world of entrepreneurship.

Their heartfelt stories are a collection that transcends boundaries, bringing to light the indomitable spirit of women who have turned setbacks into stepping stones, adversity into advantage and failures into foundations for success.

Each co-author shares an intimate narrative, offering a glimpse into the complexities of their personal and professional lives.

These are not just stories of success; they are blueprints for resilience, courage and tenacity. From navigating the intricacies of business to confronting societal expectations and personal tragedies, these women have not only weathered storms but have harnessed the power of adversity to fuel their ascent to greatness.

The Unconventional Road

Sunna Coleman
Writing & Storytelling Coach
Writers Inspired

"The only limits in our life are those we impose on ourselves."
– Bob Proctor

I don't like to be told 'no'. If I really believe in something, I find a way to do it. It may not be in the most conventional way and it may be against the odds, but I do think there is most often a way.

I wasn't always like this. There was a time when I would instantly freeze the moment someone told me I couldn't do something. I'd give up on what I wanted and say nothing about it, hoping not to cause conflict. As you can imagine, that was not a happy way to live.

So why did I do it? I grew up in a household dominated by my dad. His wrath ruled the roost and when he said 'no', there was no arguing against it. Not only that, but my mum, who came over to England from Pakistan after getting married, imposed a culture I wasn't growing up in onto me.

In Asian culture, children tend not to have much say over their choices and their parents and wider community must approve of what they do. From all angles, it seemed like I was being controlled and taught to conform no matter what.

Luckily, I didn't let this leak into my professional life. Perhaps it was my outlet when my personal life was so controlled. Maybe I only felt safe to test the boundaries out of sight of my parents.

Whatever it was, I had an unwavering belief that I could do anything I wanted and that nothing could stand in my way (one day, this self-belief and strong-will would also show up in my personal life at last).

Against cultural norms, I went to study a creative degree rather than something that would lead to a "real job" like medicine or law or accounting.

When I decided to change paths after graduating, against convention, I ended up in the top positions even though I didn't have the traditional qualifications that were apparently a "requirement". I've shared all the details of my journey through our Queens In Business book series so far.

Listing it back now, it sounds like it was somehow easy. It always seems that way in hindsight. But when you're in the thick of it, it's anything but easy. There were hundreds of setbacks along the way where you would expect anyone to just give up. But the little girl who had been told 'no' one too many times had had enough.

Instead of admitting defeat and letting my past define me, I chose resilience, and fighting against my natural instincts, societal pressures and obstacles, in order to achieve what I set out to achieve.

Just because everyone else believes you can't do it because it's not normal or seems impossible, doesn't mean it's true. You just have to be creative and find your own path to the destination. You never have to follow what's been set out before. Take the untrodden road and show them there is another way.

What's Their Secret?

One of the reasons I believe that some people are successful where others may fail or give up, is that they don't obsess over the end goal. Yes, you need a vision, but in the face of adversity, you can't keep reminding yourself of how far you are from where you need to be.

I see far too many people stop pursuing their goals because "it isn't happening fast enough" or they see no way of getting there because they don't have what's needed.

Well guess what? No one has what's needed until they gain the experience. And experience is gained over time. There is no shortcut.

When I dreamed of one day becoming a magazine editor yet had no journalism qualification or past experience, I didn't let that stop me. When I applied for thousands of internships in the hope of gaining some experience and every single one of them said 'no'... you guessed it, I didn't let that stop me! I was not about to be told 'no' from anyone else.

The key is, when the doors weren't opening for me, I created my own. I started writing anyway and posted my work on a blog so that I had something to prove that I was capable of writing great articles. That was not the way that things were done. If you wanted to become an editor you needed a journalism or English degree and you needed to have a string of work placements to support.

I took my own route. It may have been the long way round but I wasn't about to go back to university to obtain a second degree and I wasn't having any luck with the placements.

My blog took a lot of work and dedication. I read books from people who inspire me and were in the positions I would love to be in.

I researched a lot to learn how to grab attention with headlines and what successful blogs post. I took some online courses to hone my skills. I had to teach myself basic HTML so that I could make my website look great. I hate technical stuff but it was one the steps I needed to take in order to reach my end goal. There were several times where I typed in the wrong HTML code and my whole website went down. I had to spend hours on Live Chat with developers to fix issues.

It was two years in the making, while supporting myself with jobs I didn't really love, but the hard work paid off and I eventually landed my first role within journalism. "I'm finally in!" I thought. Now all I had to do was climb the ladder to the top. But even that wasn't easy.

I was looked down upon by my peers because I was unconventional. I hadn't got there the same way they had so I wasn't always favoured by those ahead of me. But my resilience got me through. No matter what tradition or society expected of me, I persevered and there's only so many people who can say 'no' if you're proving yourself to be more than capable. Someone will eventually see you.

So, instead of focusing on how unprepared or unequipped you are for where you want to be, focus on what the next logical step would be. Have zero qualifications for the position? Get training. Don't know anyone in the industry? Reach out. Think you're not good enough? Address your limiting beliefs. Whatever society or your ego throws at you in order to stop you achieving, there is an answer.

The secret is, it's all in your control if you let it be. Just keep focus on all the little things that will eventually add up to the big goal.

Action Leads To Clarity

Entrepreneurship is never a clear road. While you're in the driver seat, you're in control. But that also means you have a lot of choice in the millions of directions you could go in.

When there is so much choice and so much uncertainty, it can lead us to freeze, not knowing what step to take next in case it's the wrong one. So many fall into the trap of ruminating over options for months or even years, waiting for something to just click one day. But it rarely ever works that way.

The only way you can really discover what's right for you is by taking action. You can't think your way into gaining the experience needed to know what you want. You can only experience it and decide from there.

Action leads to results, and whether positive or negative, those results are what will help you decide if the route you chose is one you would like to continue pursuing or not. If you don't take action, you'll constantly be stuck just imagining the possibilities and moving nowhere. It's the fear of failure that holds many back. But failure is never a waste of time.

It just shows you what isn't right for you, making it clearer what might be right for you instead.

Too many entrepreneurs "fail" at something and then give up, deciding that business isn't right for them. But it's the ability to pick yourself back up from failure and learn from it that differentiates the successful ones. They are the ones that get closer and closer to their eventual end goal. Using the results of their successes and failures to help guide them rather than bring them down.

We often look at successful people and think, "Wow, how did they get so lucky?" It's not luck. It's preparation, focus and resilience that one day meet opportunity and BAM, another level is unlocked. So if you feel held back in some way or other from achieving what you dream of – whether that's judgement from friends or family, pressure from society or culture, or your inner critic – I'd like you to ask yourself: what decision would you make if nothing bad would happen?

Listen to that, and channel your resilience against the odds to bring it to life.

About Me

My life's mission is to inspire more people to turn their trauma into creativity so that they can positively impact thousands of lives. I believe that no matter what life throws at you, your resilience can pull you through and lead to more happiness and fulfilment.

Having gone through experiences in my childhood which silenced me, I am passionate about helping people express themselves, breaking the silence on things they "shouldn't say" or are afraid to share and using it to help others who are stuck or going through a difficult situation.

Through my work I have been featured in multiple international #1 best-selling books and on multiple stages alongside the likes of the BBC, ITV, C4, CNN, Disney and Warner Brothers. As an award-winning writing coach, my goal is to be by your side so that you can share your story with confidence and in the way that you intend. I believe that every voice matters and everyone has an inspiring message to share - even if you can't see it for yourself.

I dedicate this chapter to my daughter, Lyrah. May you grow up to be a strong and resilient person who can lift others up and leave this world in a better place.

You Are More Than What You See

Tanya Grant
Founder
The TNG Designs Group Limited

"I can be changed by what happens to me. But I refuse to be reduced by it."— Maya Angelou

THAT'S IT…

I'M DONE! I'm done with this business sh*t …

I don't know what I'm doing with it anymore, I'm not getting the results…

I'm over it!

Now these words might be a little different for you, but humour me, how many times have you said something like that to yourself, or spoken negatively about what it is that you do out of sheer frustration and annoyance because you've hit one too many brick walls where it's led you to a breaking point?

Be honest. How many times? Now hold that thought as here is where I'd like you to address it to quit sweeping any problems you're currently facing having around those thoughts under that lumpy carpet. It's time. Remember in my chapter in the Determined To Rise book when I asked you what needs to happen in order for you to make a change? Well that question applies here too.

And Queenie or supporter of Queenie (yes, that's you reading this right now), the theme of this 5th book in the Queens In Business book series couldn't be more timely. It nicely sums up and identifies not only the type of being that you are after having gone through any of what I've shared in the first two paragraphs here, it also nicely sums up one of the characteristics of an entrepreneur too.

I'm talking about being resilient and having resilience.

It's one of my top five skills to ensure your business keeps moving and sits alongside the likes of tenacity, persistence, perseverance, and patience.

And if you've ever looked up the actual meaning of resilience, you'll see that it describes having the capacity to withstand or to recover from difficulties "quickly" and it's not something I actually agree with. It's the word "quickly" that I have a problem with. Only because I don't think that recovering from difficulties or toughness is quick at all. I think that it requires time. I also believe that it has a major role to play in knowing that you are more than what you see too.

Now I'll be sharing more about my own experiences shortly about how I've come to realise this but know that after having read my chapter, I'll be as direct, honest, and as straight to the point as I can be when it comes to this. No, I don't know everything and wouldn't ever claim to, but what I am sure of is how I can help you to move forwards and address what's needed so that you get out of a rut that pulls you back into those "I'm done" places again... and again... and again, especially where your business is concerned.

That being said, there are a few things I need you to know to help you through this part of your journey and all you'll need to do right now is to be ready to receive what I'm about to share with you.

Ok?

Great, so let's get into it!

#1 Know To Speak Up And Talk

Now, obviously this is handy for when you speak on stages and podcasts or in interviews of any kind where you're epitomising why representation matters, but that's not what I'm referring to here. What I mean is to speak up and talk to someone, who not only shares opinions that hold value, but can also listen to how you're feeling and what you're going through.

Here's why this point is important to know.

Business as we know is many things and although there's a proverbial "I" in the word, it doesn't mean that you do it on your own, especially when we talk about managing your emotional state throughout your journey. In fact, it's my belief that business is therapy. One of the biggest reasons why those ruts I previously spoke of keep recurring is because the average entrepreneur will ignore being open or vulnerable in this kind of way in front of others. They'll perhaps view it as depositioning, overlooking or being in denial about how they're really feeling, and think that it's something that they can handle on their own.

They'll also have the tendency to think of it as a sign of another failure, or an inconvenience that they'd rather park to one side, then address later and instead of thinking of this vulnerable state as being an opportunity for building on their strength. And finally, they'll more than likely allow that state to manifest into a build-up of frustration, sadness, anxiety and feel like they're inadequate with nowhere, or even no one to turn to.

Ask me how I know this.

To say that I've only ever experienced one of these things in the past would be a complete understatement. I've faced the majority if not all of those emotions and felt that because it was my decision to put myself in business in the first place, it would be my responsibility to get myself out of the rut on my own. I didn't want to "lean" on anyone because of that feeling and, in all honesty, that was tiring, both emotionally and physically in my energy and behaviour.

So, I had to ask myself that all important question I shared with you earlier, 'what needs to happen in order for you to make a change?' And back then, even in my lowest of lows, the answers that came up for me were to speak up, talk, address those ruts being experienced and furthermore, finally being okay with asking for help.

And Queenie or supporter of Queenie, whether you're going through something similar right now, have done in the past or not at all, keep this point in your back pocket, don't ignore it.

Next...

#2 Know NOT To Get Attached To The "No"

Here's what I mean by this.

Have you ever had a time in your life where you heard a form of "no" from a prospect that one last time, so much so that every prospect you meet automatically makes you think that you're going to get a "no" from them too, even before you've given yourself the chance to say anything to them? Well, that's when you know you're attached to the word "no". It's almost like you're anchoring it to anyone you meet and when you do that, believe it or not, you're manifesting or willing it to happen.

Crazy right! But it's true and it'll be the trap that will cause you to fall into those repeated ruts, if you don't combat it by managing your state. And with that in mind, when you learn to manage your state, you'll learn to better manage your behaviour, speech, actions and levels of attachments to those "nos" too. So if you've ever been in the position where you've worked yourself up in a frenzied kind of a negative state over the potential of receiving a "no", that anxiousness, without you realising it, will show up in the conversations you're having too.

But here's the thing, you can only learn to manage your state when you understand and work through what's going on with what you've discovered about yourself in point #1.

When I was experiencing exactly this a little over a year ago before writing this chapter, those negative thoughts and attachments to "nos" were at an all-time high for me. It knocked my confidence. My certainty turned into fear and that fear or unsettled state was amplified by every word that came out of my mouth in general and especially in sales conversations. Queenie, or supporter of Queenie, I tell you the mind is one hell of a powerful thing and can at times wreak havoc on your level of certainty with what you do if you don't acknowledge and address it.

When I was going through this, aside from knowing when to speak up and talk to the right person, like I shared earlier, I began learning how to detach myself from the "no" and more importantly, I started having fun again. That's right, FUN! In fact when I think back on it, I actually started meeting my own value needs again too.

I attended networking events, and general events of interest, started speaking to more people and in doing so, my certainty came back. My brand awareness increased all whilst building better connections and what I was sharing about my business started making sense to me again. Conversations evolved into quality conversations and then transformed into something more than just a straight up "no!". They now meant results with yes's included.

Again, this all came from addressing point #1 so that this detachment could happen and incidentally that word "fun" it's actually another thing to know about learning too. Sadly, a lot of entrepreneurs forget about it and I believe it to be a case of putting too much focus on the wrong things. For example, the average entrepreneur will put all their energy and focus on the 'what's not happening', 'what's not working' or 'what's not getting paid', aspects of what they're doing, which let's face it, can take over a lot of what happens on a daily basis in the entrepreneurial world. I believe that this not only causes them to forget but also stops them from having that fun too.

#3 Know That It's All A Patience Game

Okay so now that you've familiarised yourself with the importance of knowing to speak up and talk as well as not getting attached to the "no", it's time to understand how this third and final point comes into play. Know that it's all a patience game. Those results you keep striving for, I mean. Know that although you're putting in the work right now, it doesn't necessarily mean that it'll all come to fruition straight away. That's why you have to be patient regarding it.

All too often in business, we want everything done now, answered now, responded to now dealt with now. Now. Now. Now! And whilst for the most part of the inner workings of a business, that can happen when you block out time, plan and pace yourself, it's not always the case. Especially when you try to do everything and get everything done at the same time.

And here's what I mean. When you keep saying yes to doing more work with the intention to get more in return especially when we talk of finances, which more often than not, is the result that most entrepreneurs get themselves in that repeated rut over, doing that actually can work against you rather than for you. Why? Because it creates overwhelm, which leads to burn out, which eventually leads you to feeling like you want to stop and run away from it all. It's how I felt.

I wanted to be done with it all and before I had realigned with my value needs like the one I described in point #2, that negative space I was in caused me to get into that rut of overwhelm and eventual burnout. I used to give panic responses to either my team or even to messages from clients where they would ask questions or have requests for items that weren't in the packages they've ordered, so in my haste to appease their needs, I'd respond without challenging or being curious for why they felt it was needed in the first place.

Now you're probably thinking "but Tan why is that a bad thing?" And you're right, it's not a bad thing, however saying yes like this can trip you up, especially when you're low on resources and energy in particular. Deadlines won't be met, balls will be dropped, and silly mistakes made, which can land you into an even bigger spiral of overwhelm compared to when you initially started off in the first place. That's when it's not good.

And here's what I had to learn to do… just breathe and give myself some grace. Which not only means to pause, take the pressure off your shoulders and go easy on yourself because you're doing a great job, but it also means to be patient too. Even today, I repeat this to myself. It's one of my favourite mindfulness strategy tools, and I always keep it in my back pocket.

You should too.

Because if you don't, that frustration or panic you may feel over not having achieved the target you're looking for, by the date you need to, will potentially consume you, again leading to the idea of you having to do more in order to achieve more. So, just breathe and give yourself some grace. You WILL achieve what you're striving for.

So, there you have it Queenie or supporter of Queenie, my top three things you need to know packed with some additional nuggets to help you avoid falling down into that repeated spiral of "I'm done" ruts. And here's what this all has to do with resilience and understanding that you are more than what you see: The situations that I've described as well as the emotions that were felt throughout each of these times can beat you up mentally, and at times cause you to feel like you're breaking. Knowing that there IS A WAY to move beyond those moments and how you learn to rise from them, that's what helps you come through the other side of those ruts and build your resilience.

Pay attention to the points I've shared and adapt them to your own experiences . You'll see just how resourceful you can be when it really counts, what strength you really do have, how smart you really are and just how purposeful your business actually is. You'll also discover a new version of you that will direct you to seeing that you are more than what you see.

About Me

As an award winning, solution-based brand specialist, a multiple international number one best-selling co-author, public speaker, Queens In Business Co-Founder and Founder of The TNG Designs Group Limited, I'm a huge advocate for branding and why representation matters. I've spoken on stages and many podcast interviews on the importance of these topics and how bulding up your visibility and status can have a great impact on how people see you an authority in your industry. I've worked with many SMEs as well as collaborated with global brands such as Topshop, Topman, Dorothy Perkins, and Miss Selfridge, so it's fair to say that I know what it takes for a brand to become noteworthy.

I started my career as a freelance graphic designer over 20 years ago, throughout which my past experiences have taken me through many adventures. I've witnessed a mixed bag of career driven highs and sadly demoralising lows that have included prejudices, and later, a redundancy in 2017. This became my trigger for wanting to make more of a name for myself as the go-to expert in my field, and to stop being the best kept secret. I've been able to turn what would typically feel like discouraging rejections into the movement of my greatest journey yet.

After having officially registered my business in 2019, I have since evolved into an inspiring brand specialist, motivating others to realise that they are more than what they see. Throughout my work, I instill my Group's primary values of Guide, Grounding and Growth, and it's in the Branding arm of my business, where I help business owners in the coaching space to stand out from their competition, make better connections, build better authoritative reputations all so that they can win new business more effortlessly.

One Foot In Front Of The Other

Shim Ravalia
Award Winning Business Owner
The Gut Intuition

"You may have to fight a battle more than once to win it."
– Margaret Thatcher

Have you ever had a time in your life when you've said to yourself, 'why am I doing this to myself'? On 22nd September 2018, this is exactly what I found saying to myself while climbing the mighty Ben Nevis which is arguably the highest mountain in the UK and one of the most popular as well. In 2018, I had decided to do the Three Peaks challenge which is one of the famous challenges you can do in the UK. It's basically climbing three mountains in 24 hours! Madness! What was I thinking?

My training towards the challenge was going great that year until my father passed away in June that same year so everything stopped and took a back seat so when the day finally came to climb the first mountain, I was quite nervous to say the least because deep down I knew my body just wasn't ready for such a challenge however I was raising money for a good cause so I couldn't possibly let the charity down. I wasn't on my own, thankfully, as I did it with my sister and a couple of my cousins. I dread to think how I would have done it without them.

So why am I telling you about climbing mountains? Well, the biggest thing I've learnt from climbing mountains and doing strenuous hikes up and down the country is that it's actually not that different when it comes to running a business and making changes in any areas of your life. The main aim of climbing is to get to the top of the mountain and back down again safely and in business, you want to reach the top whatever that 'top' looks like for you successfully.

What I want to share with you in this chapter is how climbing mountains helped me build a stronger mindset and resilience within myself to handle whatever challenges business, health and life has thrown at me up until this point.

The Climb

When I started the climb on Ben Nevis, it was flat and easy and I was able to have conversations with people along the way and then suddenly, the climb got very steep and my pace slowed down and I had this panic that I was going to be left behind and that I was too slow and the last one to get back down from the mountain. I compared myself to a lot of the other hikers on route and kept thinking that I was massively failing at this climb simply because my own expectations were just too high of myself. I had to go at my own pace even when I didn't want to and I had the most uncomfortable stitch you can imagine which forced me to slow down anyway so I had no choice but to. I had to not follow everyone else as their journey was different to mine. This helped me in sticking to my own lane in both of my businesses because as soon as you start comparing yourself to others, you lose focus on your own destination and getting to your own 'top' becomes frustrating, overwhelming and disordered. I like to call this destination disorder! The main thing to remember here is to always stick to your own lane.

Climbing Ben Nevis was an amazing experience with breathtaking views that just made me stop, drop and ground, taking deep breaths to fully absorb the surroundings and be present in the moment. At this point, I could no longer see the start point with my head down, slowly putting one front in front of the other and just focused on climbing. I stopped and saw just how far I've climbed even though I panicked a lot, felt overwhelmed with the big task at hand and just compared my fitness levels to everyone else. In business, you have to stop and reflect and really look at how far you've come because you can just keep going endlessly without never really looking at how much you've actually accomplished even though your own head sometimes tells you the opposite.

I finally made it to the top of Ben Nevis with my group and boy was it super cold. It was a blizzard with lots of snow and people sliding about everywhere. I couldn't even see all that well because it was chaotic and unpredictable with the weather up at the stop. I experienced four seasons in one mountain and had to change gear and clothing to suit so I could get to the top of the summit safe and sound. It's the same thing with business as sometimes you will start with a strategy and then challenges come along and you have to change the way you do things by perhaps changing the tools, strategy, or even the process. However, the destination stays the same, it's just that the road you take changes to get there.

Just When You Think It Gets Easier

I finally made it up and down Ben Nevis in one piece and you would have thought I'd be happy to be down, however I wasn't because all I could think about is that I had to now climb another mountain which was Scafell Pike. I didn't let on how much my right knee was in pain and how tired I was. I didn't want to let my group down. As it was a fair distance to get there in our private coach, I put on some tape to support my knee, deep heat to ease the aches in my lower back, food, a hot drink, and a quick nap, would see me right. Well, let me tell you it was a hit and miss.

It's 9pm in the evening and I finally arrive in Cumbria to start climbing Scafell Pike and thought to myself, 'here we go again'. Luckily, it was a clear night so not only did I have my head torch on but that evening the moon was also out so it was guiding the climb along the way as well. I'm not going to lie, this climb felt even harder even though it's smaller than Ben Nevis as the path up had a lot of big rocks to climb, which felt quite unkind on my right knee and I very quickly started to slow down. As I slowed down, my group could also see I was struggling as they were ahead and decided to help me by staying with me even though it wasn't their pace. This is similar to business when you have business partners, collaborations and team members, it's about working together and acting as a unit regardless. The biggest lesson I learnt here was to ask for help when I first realized I needed it, and not climb Scafell Pike.

However, my ego wouldn't let me as I just wanted to keep going and get two climbs done out of three done at least, and not one. I guess I was in a competition with myself and just determined to get this climb done. I finally reached the top of Scafell Pike and realized I've still got to get down.

By this point, my right knee just felt like it was shot to pieces and coming down was actually harder because of my body weight going through it. By this point one of the tour guides called Steve had to assist me the whole way down slowly but surely. I was in so much pain that he even suggested getting an air ambulance out to get me back to the bottom of the mountain. I outrightly refused and told him kindly that I'll get to the bottom no matter what because I wasn't dying and not an emergency either and that type of resource should be reserved for someone in a life threatening situation.

My body may have given up but my mind and attitude were everything on this particular climb. Positive mental attitude all day long! Remember, ask for help, don't be a martyr, get the support you need to get to where you want to go.

I made it down safely and by this point I could see dawn was approaching and it was time to climb the final mountain which was Snowden in beautiful Wales.

By this point, as a group we had missed the main coach to get to the start of Snowden. I was done and finally called it quits at this point. I had no energy left, I couldn't move my right knee or put any more weight on it. I felt defeated. I felt with my injury and being slow, I also let my group down as they could have made the final climb if it wasn't for me. They were so kind and supportive and just kept saying, 'we stick together and we don't leave each other behind no matter what'. For that I am forever grateful because having them there the whole time really helped because we laughed and played 'I spy' a lot, which in a way helped me forget about the pain I was in.

In business, you need people around that unconditionally love and support you as a unit to get through the challenges and the hard times and come out of it together by helping each other. Business may start with you but it doesn't end with just you.

We ended up getting another coach to Snowden and although we all missed the last climb, we got to see Snowden from a distance at least. I remember getting into the coach waiting to leave and just feeling completely shattered and wanting to shut my eyes and rest. I think I even went into a slight shock because I was so cold and couldn't get warm for absolutely ages. A hot chocolate was a good solution for this eventually.

Don't Let Expectations Spoil The Celebration

I finally got to a pub/cafe and just waited around for the rest of the hiking group to finish and receive our medals. I felt that the three peaks challenge broke me but it actually made me very uncomfortable thus making me a lot stronger. In fact, it stretched my thinking and brought out the strong woman I know deep down that I am and will always be.

You see, the mountains and hikes I've done since 2018 have taught me a lot about life and business. It's funny how an activity that has nothing to do with your usual day to day business activities can teach you so much about business itself.

I sat in that pub/cafe going into deep reflection that actually, I am not defeated because I am quite a competitive person and of course I would have loved to have gone back home having done all three mountains in 24 hours rather than two but it was what it was. I remember making a promise to myself that I would come back the following year and complete Scafell Pike and Snowden with my group but do it in our own way without the pressure of completing it within 24 hours.

Guess what? I did! I completed both mountains in a respectable amount of time over a weekend without an ache in my body because we rested overnight in a hotel and off we went again the following day to climb another mountain.

For me, that worked so well and still does to this day. Relating this to business, I've learned that you can create your own flow with how you run your business and how you get your ideas to come to fruition, don't follow what everyone else is doing.

To truly build resilience within yourself and for your business is to understand the following:

- That the path you take to where you want to go is always going to be uneven, uncertain and simply uncomfortable. The main thing is take each day as it comes and one step at a time no matter how big or small those steps are. A small step forward is huge progress in my world than no step forward at all.

- Don't look up miles ahead and look back down like I did on the mountains to try and discourage yourself from the journey. Stop, breathe and just appreciate how far you've actually come.

- Finally, there are no shortcuts to this journey other than to keep moving forward...

One foot in front of the other, always!

About Me

I am the Founder of The Gut Intuition and Co Founder for Queens In Business. I help business owners and entrepreneurs go from stress to unlimited energy and razor sharp focus without burning out in health and in business.

I've had the pleasure of being featured in many well-known publications like Business Woman Today, CBS News, Fox, NBC and ABC to really spread my message and my vision about health for the future of entrepreneurs all over the world. Most recently, my company was recognised to be the best health and wellbeing facility in Greater London too.

Born and bred in East London, and coming away from university with two degrees in Sports Rehabilitation and from here I worked in gyms and leisure centres until I found my entrepreneurial path.

Having been an entrepreneur for over 12 years now, I have had my strength and resiliency tested so many times and have always come out to the other side of it stronger than before. I hope that this book gives you the courage and fire to keep going when times do get difficult and know that it's just temporary, knowing you will come out of it a different, stronger version of you ready to take on whatever comes your way.

Stop Hiding, Start Inspiring

Chloë Bisson
Multi-Award Winning Speaker,
Podcast Host, and Publisher
Inspired By

"The power to inspire resides in being visible, sharing your message, and embracing vulnerability without a mask on."
– Chloë Bisson

It was April 2022.

I was lying on a sun lounger, looking out over the beautiful views of Coral Bay in Cyprus. Taking in the fresh sea air and feeling the heat of the sun on my skin.

I had been running my first retreat in Cyprus and as we were finishing the retreat, I took some time out to sit in the sun and catch up with a good friend of mine. She'd been a client of mine for years after we published her first book in 2020 and had come on this retreat to reflect and strategise the upcoming year.

We were talking about all the big plans we both had and I was telling her about all the opportunities coming up for me.

I started my business in 2017 and after hitting multiple six figures in my business, growing a great team and feeling like "I'd made it", I had decided to scale back and transition my role into a trainer. Speaking had always been my biggest passion and as I'd spoken in front of hundreds of people internationally in my business, it was fairly easy to train on behalf of other companies.

I absolutely loved it because I didn't have to worry about marketing, posting on social media, managing a big team or getting clients. All I had to do was show up and deliver. It was a dream!

I'd already built a strong team in the book publishing company and we had regular referrals so even in that business, I didn't have to actually worry about getting new clients.

It was fairly stable, secure and, to be honest with you, I thought it was pretty great.

And as I was telling her all of the updates of what had happened, she had a blank look on her face and said:

"Chloe, why are you hiding behind these companies? Why are you playing small?"

I was speechless.

It was not what I had expected her to say at all.

I was expecting her to say all the usual things that people had said to me in the past:

"Wow what a great opportunity!"

"It's amazing being able to just show up and get clients given to you!"

"Sounds like a dream!"

But her reaction was totally different.

I was shocked.

When I asked her what she meant, she explained that she knew I was meant for more and that I could help so many more people if I stop playing small or taking the easy option.

I didn't realise it at the time but I had given in and chosen to stay where it was comfortable.

Being Too Comfortable Is Dangerous

For as long as I can remember I've craved stability in my life and so, like in any business, when I had moments of "oh sh*t! How am I going to pay the bills?!" my need for stability and security were really challenged. So, when I was offered the opportunity to train for other training companies without these worries and I felt comfortable, it felt like a dream come true.

But in reality, being too comfortable can be dangerous too. When we're too comfortable, we're not being challenged, we're not being stimulated and therefore, we're not growing.

And with living things, like us, there are only two options, growing or dying. It sounds harsh but it's true.

Think of a plant. If you water and feed it, it grows. If you don't water and feed it for a long enough period of time, it starts to wilt and die.

And this is a very risky position to be in.

Instead, in order to grow, develop and build our resilience, it's important to challenge ourselves and push ourselves out of our comfort zone.

Whilst this can seem scary, I found it becomes A LOT easier when you surround yourself with people who are also pushing themselves out of their comfort zone and being resilient too.

Even if you're not feeling ready to do it yet, it comes with learned behaviour and being around people who are stretching and challenging themselves can help you to learn it and believe that you can do it too. It makes it feel more "normal" and staying still and being too comfortable becomes the "strange" option.

But back in Cyprus, I was still quite happy to be comfortable and I hadn't realised the issue with it. I was surrounded by people who admired the fact that I was training for these companies, not people that challenged me about it, until now.

Yet me being my usual determined and stubborn self, I heard what my friend had said to me but I didn't take any notice and kept justifying to myself what I was doing was the best thing for me.

I got back to the UK and straight into a meeting with one of the companies I was training for and something really strange happened.

I didn't feel the same love and passion for what I was doing anymore.

At one point I thought it might just be the holiday blues and that it would pass but it was way more than that.

Every time I had a meeting for my own business with a book publishing client, I felt energised and excited and yet when I trained for other companies, I felt empty.

I realised that the safety and stability I'd gained from training for other companies had dampened my passion and drive for success and growth.

And I realised I'd been hiding.

I'd been hiding behind people who could take the risks instead of me.

The risk of no one buying
The risk of not being able to pay their bills
The risk of bad press
The risk of being judged

They were all risks that they were having to face and as an external trainer, I didn't have to worry about any of that.

But by hiding from that, I'd also been hiding from being visible, sharing my message and inspiring people without a mask on.

Risks, Returns and Resilience

Building your brand, sharing your message and inspiring others is an amazing mission and hugely fulfilling and in order to do that, you need to put yourself out there. But what no one prepares you for is that, with every possibility of inspiring people, there is also the possibility of getting unwanted attention, unwanted feedback and negative opinions.

In order to build any business, we all know we need to market ourselves but when it comes to *really* inspiring people, whether it's through telling your story, speaking on stages, speaking on podcasts or writing your book, it's a whole different level of visibility and with it, vulnerability.

It's vital to accept that if you want to inspire people, you'll need to build yourself a piece of armour to deal with the negativity that you may attract. You don't need to wear the armour all the time, just have it with you when you need it. I see this armour as part of my resilience toolbox.

To me, resilience is about putting yourself out there despite the risk of negativity or repercussions. Being resilient enough to do it anyway because you know, deep down, that the benefit of you sharing your message, stepping into the spotlight and inspiring people is worth it.

I used to think that I had to be "strong" to be a female entrepreneur and show up a "strong independent woman" otherwise people wouldn't value me but I couldn't have been more wrong.

The more vulnerable you are, the more people will be inspired by you and the more they will value you.

In the same way, as an entrepreneur, the more risks you take, the more resilience you build and the more returns you get, whether it's in the form of money, freedom or fulfilment.

Whilst I knew I'd been avoiding taking those risks and avoiding the fears, I knew I would have to face them if I was going to walk away from the safety and security of speaking for another company and instead start sharing my own voice again.

I'd always had a dream to inspire people but how could I possibly inspire people if I was hiding behind someone else, if I was wearing a mask.

It was at this moment I realised I had to stop hiding and start inspiring.

Logistically it wasn't actually that hard to do given that I already had a profitable book publishing business that had been publishing books whilst I was training for other companies.

But mentally and emotionally, it was definitely not as easy and that's where doubt really started to creep in.

"What will everyone think?"
"What will people say?"
"What will I say if people ask me?"

I couldn't help but worry about what people would think and the doubt began to take over.

Doubt Kills More Dreams Than Failure Ever Will

Often when we're about to embark on something incredible, that little voice of fear can kick in to make us question if it's the right thing to do, especially if you've experienced that challenge before.

Many fears are irrational, where you are afraid of something that you've never experienced before.

For example, many people are afraid of dying, yet have never died before. These fears are based on the assumption of what it might be like if it were to happen. But the hardest fear to overcome is a fear that is based on things you've actually experienced, pains you've already felt and are afraid to feel again.

In my situation, I'd already been a successful business owner and had all of the challenges which was why I had unconsciously chosen to play small because it was easier than facing the fears.

But here's the thing. Those fears and that little voice inside of your head often shows up at times when you need to take the action the most.

That little voice is part of your ego that's trying to keep you safe. Our egos are there to keep us alive and so when it notices that we're about to take a leap of faith, something new, exciting and even possibly dangerous, that voice will show up to hold us back.

What I've learnt over the last seven years in business is that every time I'm about to start a new, exciting and yet very unknown journey and that voice shows up, it's ended up being the best thing I've ever done.

You just need to lean into it.

The one piece of advice I'd give when you can feel the fear kicking in is to be mindful of what you're focusing on. If you're feeding your brain with negative fear-based thoughts then it is going to be harder to be resilient and push through the challenges. That's like putting the wrong fuel in a car and trying to drive it.

Instead, you can challenge your thoughts with What If Thinking.

What If Thinking is where you notice a fear or thought and challenge it with the opposite What If.

For example:

My Thought: "What if people think I'm not good enough to do it on my own?"

What If Thinking: "What if people are excited that I've FINALLY done it and say I should have done it sooner?!"

This approach helps you to challenge the fear based thoughts with other possibilities, taking the power out of your fear based thought.

So when you're pushing yourself out of your comfort zone and putting yourself out there, just remember that the voice is there to keep you safe and you don't have to go from one extreme to the other.

Taking The Mask Off and Showing Up

When I started my journey back to being the face of my business and showing up 100% as myself, I didn't go from zero to 100 straight away.

On 3rd May 2022, I started doing a daily Facebook Live every weekday morning with the goal to just get comfortable with showing up again. I called it Coffee With Chloë and I had no idea where it would go, I just wanted to take my mask off and start showing up as myself. Three years on and I still go live every morning at 8am UK time.

I then started showing up in my business again, putting myself out there to speak at events and share my message about our book publishing services.

Up until that point, we'd published 15 bestselling books, yet hardly anyone knew about us. Considering I'm a marketing expert, it had been the world's best kept secret but not anymore.

It was then that Inspired By Publishing was born.

Within a couple of months, we'd taken on more clients, we were working on more books that we'd ever managed before and people started to know who we were. We became one of the UK's fastest growing book publishing companies and it felt incredible.

Finally, I felt like myself again; sharing my message and inspiring people to show up and be heard.

And I was only just getting started.

On 26th June 2023, I launched the Inspired By Show where I interview entrepreneurs, celebrities, authors, industry leaders, speakers and anyone who has an inspiring message they want to share and take the mask off.

At the time of writing this, we've published 38 bestselling books and worked with 77 bestselling authors and co-authors to share their inspiring stories in books.

And the most incredible part is that I still work closely with many of the companies I used to train for and I still train with them today. But this time I get to show up with my brand and my content, with the mask off.

If you have a mission and purpose to inspire others, then it's time to stop hiding and start inspiring.

You owe it to yourself AND to the people that need to hear your message.

I know it seems scary and to be honest with you, it IS scary.

But that's where resilience kicks in. Each time you deal with a challenge, you're building your ability to handle the next one.

Because, in my opinion, resilience isn't something that you can be taught. It's something you learn from experience. I wish I could tell you how to become more resilient in these three simple steps but it's not possible.

The only way to become more resilient is by living, breathing and experiencing things that make you grow. It's like trying to become fluent in a language without ever going to that country or actually speaking to anyone in the language.

You need to experience it to learn it.

We all have to face challenges and the more you put yourself out there and push yourself out of your comfort zone, the more challenges you'll have to face.

But I know with the experience I've gained from my own challenges, I've built the resilience to face anything that comes my way.

I'll forever keep pushing myself to the next level in life and business and to any challenge that comes up on the way... bring it on!

About Me

If there is only one thing you need to know about me, it is this – I believe that all women have what it takes to be successful female entrepreneurs and that women have the right to create their own businesses, their own income streams and their own happiness.

I'm a three-time number one best-selling author, an international speaker, multi-award winning entrepreneur and Co-Founder of the Queens In Business Club.

As a chartered accountant at the age of twenty-one and director by the age of twenty-four, my life came to a sharp halt when I was diagnosed with severe clinical depression at the age of twenty-five. After months of growth and recovery, I knew I was meant for more than just the normal path and began my journey of entrepreneurship… little did I know how much of a journey it would really be!

Since then, I've been featured on the cover of Global Woman Magazine, spoken on stage alongside Kim Kiyosaki and have been featured on BBC, Fox, ABC, NBC, CW, London Business Magazine, Business Woman Today, Foundr and more.

Today, Chloë runs multiple six figure businesses, including a book publishing business that helps entrepreneurs to become bestselling authors and a global training organisation that teaches entrepreneurs how to grow their visibility and build their authority in the media.

With all of her businesses, her passion and purpose is the same; to help people to reach their full potential using what they already have, whether it's scaling their business, growing their brand or monetising their story.

Diamond In The Storm

Angela Haynes-Ranger
Award Winning Writer & Style Coach
Adourable

"The greatest glory in living lies not in never falling, but in rising every time we fall." – Nelson Mandela

Standing here, I can't believe how far I've come. Over the years, the challenges came thick and fast and I must admit there was a time when I wasn't at all confident how things would turn out. I guess we can never really be sure, but I'm proud. Proud that I dug deep and weathered the storm. That I believed in my dream but more importantly, believed in myself, my vision and my values. The journey has made me stronger, more aligned with who I am, what I stand for and who I aspire to be.

The day began like any other, with the hustle and bustle of getting the kids ready for school. My mornings felt like a well-choreographed dance, a delicate balancing act between the demands of my family and the looming responsibilities of my career. But the routine was my anchor, providing me with a level of normalcy amidst the chaos that lay ahead.

My partner's sudden illness had cast a shadow over our lives. What started as a normal day had unfolded into a narrative that no one in the family had been prepared for.

I remember having to navigate the journey to long hospital visits, medical consultations, and the emotional rollercoaster of watching a loved one deteriorate, whilst also seeing them slip away, having to continue keeping things afloat, being strong for everyone else and keeping the family together, whilst still having to function on a day to day basis.

The demanding nature of my career showed no mercy and for that period, all I could do was compartmentalise my emotions and focus on the tasks at hand. Meetings, deadlines, and expectations became a relentless tide that nearly threatened to engulf me. Yet, in the eye of the storm, I discovered a mountain of strength I never knew I possessed.

I had been slowly following my dream of building a successful business but it was proving hard. The evenings blurred into a mass of responsibilities. My partner now faced a diagnosis that left us both shocked and numb. Cancer had cast its shadow over our lives, and as treatments began, he underwent a transformation that shook the foundation of our relationship as he became a person we hardly recognised. His personality changed, he became angry, he lashed out and we all paid the price.

In life, we all encounter storms, turbulent winds, and unexpected downpours. Yet, it is the strength within us that enables us not just to weather the storm but to emerge from it stronger, wiser, and more powerful than ever. Those difficult times really helped to shape me, and changed my perspective on life for the better. It's important to strive for the things that are important to you, live your life and never underestimate what you can achieve no matter the mountain you have to climb.

Learning The Lessons

Growing up, I was predominantly surrounded by women. My circle consisted of mainly strong women, all of whom I took daily lessons from and learnt a lot about life. I was always fascinated with finding out more about their lives, what their aspirations were and learning from their experiences.

Thankfully, unlike many of the women I encountered, I had always been brought up to believe that I was as good as anyone else and could achieve anything I put my mind to regardless of the narrative of others. I'm thankful that I was brought up with that solid foundation of knowing and believing in myself. To be honest, I don't think I would have pursued many of the things that I did and been successful at them, if this hadn't been the case. I don't think I would have really known myself, what I wanted and what I definitely did not want. In hindsight, I'm glad that I have pursued those things. They helped to shape my thinking and my actions even to this day. I guess this is where my deep passion for helping women grew.

Setbacks Are Not Roadblocks

As an entrepreneur, that pull within me was an important one. It was the thing that would keep me going when times were hard, when the path to take was not so apparent and the doubts and insecurities raised their ugly heads. Along my journey I learnt that it is not just about merely bouncing back from adversity; but it's the art of transforming challenges into stepping stones for my own personal growth. That flame within you, that fire that refuses to be extinguished by even the harshest of words or of life's lived experiences. That is your resilience, a force that can withstand the fiercest storms. I believe as women, we have an innate ability to tap into this source, connect with our passions and turn adversity into opportunity. It's about understanding that setbacks are not roadblocks but rather just a detour, leading to unexpected, yet beautiful, destinations.

Building my business gave me a deeper insight into this. It gave me the perfect opportunity to hear women's experiences first hand, and the ways in which they usually felt they couldn't really be themselves. Many felt they were just going through life wearing a mask, living through a false self: more concerned about keeping the peace and pleasing others than being true to themselves. Many times they experienced a feeling of emptiness, often feeling they had to keep these feelings of lack and insecurities to themselves. They didn't feel comfortable sharing their feelings and vulnerabilities with their friends, families or even their husbands.. Many struggled with a lack of self worth and had low self esteem, either because that was how they had always perceived themselves, or for many, that was how they had always been made to feel. I knew I could help these women, I wanted to. I felt deeply connected to them. I wanted them to feel confident, self-assured and empowered, regardless of what the external world was telling them. In hindsight, I think this is how I always felt even growing up. I didn't see limits, I didn’t dwell on limitations, I just knew what I wanted, aspired to get it, then worked hard to achieve it.

On The Journey

I always knew I wanted to be an entrepreneur. The idea of working solely for someone else for the rest of my life always filled me with both panic and dread. I had no doubt that I was going to do things differently from many of my peers... However, this didn’t always go down well. Initially, I felt that I was expected to follow the traditional path and work for an employer just like most other people did, but I refused to take on that narrative. I knew whatever I did had to light me up, had to really connect with me in some way as well as make a difference to the lives of others. I had to be aligned to my purpose.

Helping women to look good came very naturally to me. I had always been a lover of fashion and everyone told me I had a real eye for it, but for me it was more than that. It was about connecting with women who wanted to feel better about themselves. Those who felt disconnected but didn't have the tools or belief to navigate themselves to a better place. Over time, I had the privilege to work in some very exciting places and meet many interesting women. From VIPs, celebrities to the ordinary woman next door and what I came to realise is, they all shared the same fundamental insecurities, fears and challenges that we all do, and that at some point, I certainly did too.

I knew that I wanted to build a community where women felt both safe and heard. I was exposed to a diversity of women, all with their own intriguing experiences and stories to tell. From having a lack of confidence, experiencing racism, living with narcissistic abuse or the challenges of trying to be the best partner and mother they aspired to be and almost everything else in between. Their stories and experiences made me determined and focused to help regardless of the many challenges I faced.

To be honest, I always had what some might describe as a secure and somewhat privileged life, but here I was getting my first lessons in resilience from these amazing women. It helped me to see things differently. I took the skills and experience I had and used it to make a real difference and to make an impact. Yes, it's great to look good, and that was my initial path into coaching women, but it was no longer just about that as it had been when I first started my entrepreneurial journey. It was about much more… a deeper meaning, a deeper understanding of how much of a difference it can make to help elevate someone's self worth and self esteem, and the impact that can have in all areas of someone's life. I'm proud to say I have seen it, the growth, the positive change in direction, the real connection back to self for many women, feeling good about themselves again… and for me, that's priceless!

There were many challenges to becoming an entrepreneur although I never doubted what I wanted to achieve. I was always confident in my abilities but soon realised that the opinions of others, their comments and their usually subdued actions, spoke volumes. It was not always what was openly said, but on many occasions it was what wasn't said that could have had an effect on my own confidence. Initially I was doing well, following my passion and happy with life, but soon began to realise that not everyone was particularly supportive or happy with my exuberance for life, or my "I can do it!" attitude, particularly when they started to see some evidence of success.

I was already challenged from a time perspective, having a young family, juggling a demanding job whilst trying to get a business off the ground, a situation I'm sure many of you can relate to. Add to that mix an obstructive and less than supportive boss, my father's sudden illness and a cancer diagnosis for my partner and we potentially had a perfect cocktail for stress, depression and burnout.

The Importance Of You

Everyone always told me that I was fortunate to know what my passions were and what I wanted to do in life. Being in my own little world took up the majority of my spare time. I loved everything that I was doing. I spent many hours building the business, networking and making great connections... but to pretend it was easy would be a lie. It wasn't easy. I worked really hard and made a lot of sacrifices in both time, health and money. I was always taught to work hard and I can achieve anything and that's the mindset I adopted. I still believe this, but I must stress that the most important thing is to look after YOU. Don't make the mistake of always putting yourself last on your list of priorities... as without you, your health and your wellbeing, what do you really have?

To help prevent stress and experiencing burnout, I would always set myself a goal, a time frame and devise a plan on how I would get there. I was always focused on the outcome and put a plan in place to help overcome any challenges. I knew that things would not always be easy, I'd experienced enough to humble myself in that regard, and realised that sometimes you just need to be patient with yourself, be consistent and stay committed. You may also need to accept that sometimes not everyone will be on board with your vision, so you may have to walk all or part of the journey alone.

Looking back, I can see how easy it could have been to have my confidence slowly eroded by those around me. Whenever I reached a new level of the vision or a new opportunity arose for the business, I was of course super excited, sharing my news with anyone who would listen including friends and family. I was excited to know that I was successfully helping women to improve their confidence and had also helped them to elevate their personal brand. Sadly, I noticed that good news was not always supported and sometimes wasn't even acknowledged. I did notice however, that I did receive acknowledgement or sometimes comments for things which could be classed more as negative like when I had been let down, or things didn't quite go to plan. What does that say about human nature? To tell the truth, I found that sad. Some people only wanted to comment from a place of negativity. There's another important lesson I learnt — surround yourself with likeminded people and those who are there to support and uplift you. Doing this will make a world of difference to your entrepreneurial journey and in fact your personal journey too. I've tried it and believe me, things have changed for the better. Find your tribe, your own supportive community where you can not only grow, but positively thrive.

Stepping Up

Whilst working towards my goals, I knew I had to step outside of my comfort zone. I had to listen to my intuition and just go for it, no matter what…

There are real challenges to overcome when building a business, and for me one of the biggest, was building a business alongside a legal career. Like with everything, I tried to do my best. I knew I would have to try to balance the demands of a job as well as follow my dream. One of the most difficult things I had to overcome was working with a boss that constantly tried to make my life a misery and that's how it really felt. On reflection, I think she was very insecure, and I suspect quite unhappy with life. This alongside the long hours and demanding work actually helped to build my stamina and gave me fuel to strive to be my own success story. It helped me to work harder towards achieving my goals, as well as increase my skill set, and turn a negative situation into a positive one… a great thing for business… right?

Although I felt confident, I was definitely a people pleaser. I don't know why, but I always felt uncomfortable when faced with potentially awkward situations. I had confidence personally, when it came to what I wanted, my own ambitions and my goals, but found it difficult to set boundaries for myself with others in fear of letting them down or upsetting them usually to the detriment of myself. "Keep the peace"', "Just do it, it's easier" was usually the voice I heard in my head. Yes, in some situations that may be true, but as the saying goes "you can't pour from an empty cup" and I began to learn this pretty fast. So, I had to adopt a new mindset, regardless of other people's objectives. I had to start setting boundaries and to look after ME!

I continued to work hard and my business grew. I was being invited to take part and speak at events both in the UK and abroad and collaborate with other businesses. The momentum was building and I was loving it! Being able to network with like minded people and other entrepreneurs and to connect with women who needed my help, was all the confirmation I needed that I was in the right place, doing the right thing, bringing value to the lives of women and growing a great network and community. I'm aligned with what I do and love the women I get to serve.

As you read this chapter, take some time to think back. Have you ever had a time when you truly thought you couldn't overcome something and you totally surprised yourself? Well… that was me and I have no doubt it could be you too… trust and believe in yourself. You have everything you need within!

These storms have shaped my life in profound ways, leaving lessons that will forever mark my journey and are now part of my story.

Let this chapter be a call to action for you. A call for you to embrace YOUR story and to recognise that resilience is not the absence of struggle but the triumph over it. I can now boldly share mine with authenticity, with passion and with clarity, to help women who need a safe space to reconnect, and to confidently do it in style! Through our shared stories and collective strength, I hope to inspire, uplift, and empower both you and women globally, on your own exciting journey.

This chapter is dedicated to my very special parents who always led by example, instilled great values, and provided me with all the love, kindness and stability I needed in my life. And to my two beautiful souls, Lauren and Ashleigh, who inspire me every day and are the greatest gifts a mother could ever wish for.

About Me

Award Winning Style Coach & Writer, Best-Selling Co-Author, Speaker, Founder of Adourable and Director at Queens In Business.

With a real passion for what she does and a wealth of expertise, Angela is the Founder of Adourable, and is dedicated to empower, educate and inspire women and to give them the tools they need to look good, feel great, reclaim their confidence and positively impact their lives.

Having gone through an extremely challenging and life changing period whilst also navigating the world of family, career and business, Angela now uses her experience, knowledge and expertise to help women on a journey of self-discovery and personal growth; helping them to elevate their personal brand and to understand that they are truly the master navigator of their own lives.

Angela is also an Assistant Editor at Queens In Business Magazine and best-selling book series, as well as an Executive Contributor at Brainz Magazine, where she recently received the Brainz CREA Global Award 2023 which is awarded to top entrepreneurs, influential leaders and innovators. She has also worked with brands such as Estee Lauder, Harrods, Harvey Nichols and Selfridges.

Follow YOUR Light Within

Laura Meredith
Director
Ryedaura Ltd

"Hold your dreams tight and follow your light within."
– Laura Meredith

Hi, I'm Laura Meredith and I run a successful six figure bookkeeping and executive assistant business.

Prior to starting the business in 2021, just after the lockdowns of Covid-19, I was working full time in a similar role and had been for the majority of my career.

Every position I had ever held, was never for more than five years at a time, there was always a light within me that wanted to do more and have something I could call my own. Now, don't get me wrong, I loved my jobs, even waitressing and bar work which is where I first started, the desire to provide a high level of customer service, which was something I strived for.

Although I wanted to start my own business, I hadn't a clue where to begin. What would I do? Would I be good enough? Why would anyone buy from me? What would I do if it all went wrong? I had a small family and we relied upon my earnings monthly to pay the bills and get by, so if things went wrong, how would we survive?

With all this swishing around in my mind, I truly couldn't see a way forward, which is when I decided to try and make a hobby of mine into a business, making celebration cakes. For a couple of years, I did this as a side business to my day job, along with attending fairs and exhibitions at weekends to sell cake slices. It didn't last long, which was not because it was very hard work, stressful and long hours but more so that I couldn't seem to make a profit.

Customers always thought it was just flour and eggs and therefore a cake that I'd spent upwards of - eight hours on, baking, icing and decorating with handmade sugar flowers etc should only be worth £35-35. It was highly unlikely that I made more than £2 per hour for myself, per cake. The cake stall however did a little better, but trying to make and store the quantities needed in a home kitchen and then sell all goods on the day as they were perishable proved difficult indeed. So, I came to the realisation that this was not working at all, I couldn't seem to make a profit and see a way forward as a viable business and I'd lost all love for my hobby of sugar-craft and baking.

I saw this as a huge failure, if I couldn't make baking work as a business, how would I ever succeed at anything else. What was I doing so wrong, how does anyone ever make a go of things? The fear within grew stronger and started to consume the light within telling me I had more to give. So I carried on as normal, head down and got on with my job but the battle in my head continued.

This fear that I wasn't good enough, which was deeply ingrained in me from my childhood, along with the advice from family and friends of "keep your head down girl and work hard, you'll be alright then", alright was safe, and safe having a young family was what I wanted most. At this point in my life I had a husband and a young son. My parents had both passed away to chronic illnesses, along with my grandparents and year on year I was losing more distant family members this way too. It was like the net was closing in on me and I longed for safety and security.

Unexpected Turns

Then, Covid-19 shook the world; my safe job began to wobble, there was mention of furlough (what even did that word truly mean). It made me worry what would happen, I had no control over the company I worked for, my job could be at risk. How were we ever going to pay the bills if I lost my job now, who would employ me in these times? Looking back, I had nothing to fear with my role, I quickly took some of our daily activities online and I had the best director, who always treated me as an equal and worked through the whole pandemic with me side by side. Totally unexpectedly, it was my husband who was furloughed; for a few weeks. This was a relief as at this point we understood more of what this meant, and it was an opportunity for us to homeschool our son and still have an income. Things seemed to be going well, as a family without the school runs and rat race to and from work. Our lives were quieter, we got to spend lots of family time together, we baked bread in the morning and sat in the garden to have our lunch. We were safe in our home but things were about to change.

During a standard weekly call, my husband was made redundant. I remember him telling me the news and for a moment I didn't believe it, or more like I didn't want to believe it was true. Running through my mind was the fear of what we would do now, how would we cope, good jobs were nonexistent during this time, I was completely numb. We spent weeks applying for new jobs for him, close to 300 when we found him something warehouse based, not ideal but it would keep us afloat for now.

With him being unhappy at work, working shifts and missing all special family days like birthdays, Christmas and bank holidays, we knew something had to change and fast, so I made him a promise. I promised that if he stuck at this new role for 18 months max, I'd start a new business for us that would be able to employ us both full time. Looking back, I was terrified, what had I just promised, how on earth was I ever going to deliver on this, what was I going to sell or service to provide and where was I supposed to start! Going back to the cakes was a thought that entered my mind but I looked at the numbers night after night and realised this was not an option.

A couple of months past and desperation was setting in but I had to uphold my part of the bargain and let's face it, it was something I'd dreamed of, having my own business, a legacy for our son, being in control of the direction of the business at all times, I had to pull this off.

Taking The Leap

One night I was scrolling on social media and I saw an advert for a free online webinar about starting your own business, so totally out of my comfort zone I booked a place and attended. The host was superb, a really positive person that gave solid advice. He suggested if you are unsure of what to do, then initially, stick to what you know and are good at. For me that's bookkeeping and organisation, I'd done this my whole career (and life) so why try to do anything different.

At the end of the webinar, we were invited to pay a small fee of £99 for a half day in-person session with the host, to learn more on starting a business and being successful at it. At the time, this was a lot of money to us and buying online like this scared me as I was wary of scammers and falling into peoples sales funnels. I'd have to use annual leave to attend, plus to top it all off, the session would be held nearly four hours away from my home. I remember thinking, do I take a chance, and step out of my comfort zone or is this too risky? So I decided to give it a go, okay we stood to lose money but we could also gain, this person was inspirational, he seemed to have business success and was offering some golden nuggets on how to succeed in business.

While attending the training session, I met some really great individuals, had some wonderful positive conversations with people that thought alike and learnt a lot, things I would not have considered myself and it was there I booked myself onto a four day business school course.

The dread inside me signing the paper to agree to make a further payment was immense, this wasn't just my money, it was my husbands too but I had to follow the light within and believe, plus the credit card eased the transaction, meaning I had two years to pay it off! I needed to stop thinking of the "what ifs" and go with it, believe to achieve. The next challenge that lay before me, before attending the business school, was to get clear in my head how I was going to make my bookkeeping and administration services into a business. I knew I had to bury the doubt, stay positive and true, then things would be okay. The reality of doing this was however not as easy as it sounded!

As the weeks went by, I took to the internet for some extensive market research, after which things became much clearer. Staying true to myself, I knew I wanted to offer a great service to all clients, giving them excellent return on investment and offering top class bookkeeping and administration services. My research had concluded that this was known as being a "virtual assistant" something I'd not come across before but

I'd now found it was becoming more popular all over the world since the pandemic.

So, the week of the business school came, I packed my suitcase, kissed my family goodbye and set off on my travels, gosh I was so nervous. Hoping this would not be a waste of time and money, that I would be able to make a go of things for us all, I'd be bright enough to understand, not making a fool of myself and above all honour my promise. As the cherry on top of the cake, I hated leaving home, my joy is always closing the door to the house and locking the world outside but for four very long days, there'd be nowhere to hide!

Boy, they were long days indeed, each day was between 8-10 hours of full on learning. Hour by hour more new material and ways of working were presented to us, plus there was homework too, but oh my goodness was it worth it. It will forever be one of the best experiences of my life. I made new friends, excellent business contacts and gained such valuable business knowledge.

During my time there, one of the hosts asked "what's the goal for you Laura, what do you really want?" For me, that was simple, I've always wanted to do more and give back, the ideal of having a business that can support my family, provide an exemplary service to clients and in turn begin to allow us to embark on the life we've dreamt of is something I've been longing for all my life. But, the purpose, would be for the business to provide all these things and create a little surplus income, so we could start something special, a little smallholding, that could give animals a safe and loving home and allow us to offer free holidays to families who have a parent suffering with cancer, giving them all a chance to have a holiday, away from daily life, a place to relax and unwind and escape the walls around them.

One of the most important things I learnt, after doing an exercise within the class, was that I am the only person holding myself back. My beliefs, made up from past experiences, failures and peoples advice over the years were suffocating the women within. Causing me to second guess, doubt myself all the time and drown out the light. I then decided to make myself a promise for once, to do all I could to prevent this going forward, begin to listen to my intuition and believe in myself. I returned home to smiling faces and the most amazing of cuddles, it was great to be back and I was so inspired by the course, the following morning, I set about getting everything in motion.

Putting Plans Into Action

Firstly we had to think of a business name, it needed to be something to show we are a family business, timeless and traditional, like our values. I suddenly thought back to our long walks during the pandemic evenings, through the local forests and over the fields we would go, chatting all the way to each other. During these walks, we were thinking of names for our dream home and came up with Ryedaura (Ryan, our son, Edward my husband and Laura, myself). Although this was a business and not a dream home, when I suggested it to everyone, we agreed it was perfect and like it was meant to be.

Sitting at the dusty old family desktop PC, I quickly incorporated the company online and set up a business bank account; after the outlay of the course, we'd just £200 to spare, so my husband and I agreed to use this for the business. We enlisted a local IT company to help us get the old PC up to scratch and set about creating our first website.

Still having two full time jobs between us, we spent the next few weeks getting the systems and processes in place to allow us to support clients efficiently, making sure we had a fully functioning website displaying our services and I took to the internet for some CPD. The only problem was that we had no clients but thanks to the course, I had learnt of the many ways to put ourselves out there, to see if anyone needed some help. Although I have to say, I wasn't convinced all of them were for me, I'm not a front and centre of the party kind of person, so naturally preferred the options based on more softer relationship building first, before any hard selling commenced.

Then, I received a text message that was about to change everything; it was from someone I'd met on the course, who wanted to enlist our services for help with their business. I couldn't quite believe it and in true Laura style I proceeded totally cool and calm on the exterior but inside I was buzzing! Then I received another message and before I knew it, within the space of a very few short days, I'd secured three clients. I was ecstatic, I was really doing this, honouring my promise to myself and that to my husband.

What proceeded to follow was my biggest juggling act of all time. Suddenly I was juggling my full time job, the new business, being a mum to our son and a wife to my husband. However, it somehow didn't seem like work, supporting my own clients was different in some way, a joy to know I was able to provide an efficient, effective and exemplary service at all times and was fully in the driving seat.

I won't lie, the next few months were relentless, working every hour possible, juggling family life with work and the business and trying not to drop a ball in any area was not easy at all. However within four months, I was finally able to deliver on my promise to my husband, the business had grown and was now able to support him full time.

The next hurdles we faced were choosing our team members, as we grew the business further, the desire had always been to have a small but mighty team, providing a really nice place to work, as let's face it, we spend a large part of our lives at work. It was key to find people who shared the same values as us, skills can be taught but values are engrained deep within us.

Growing the business further was then the natural next stage. As I mentioned before, I'm not into the "hard sell", so I needed to make a softer approach work for me. I quickly understood and I believed more in "serving" and not "selling", so this was something I held onto tightly. I began to look at how I'd found my current clients and realised I'd either had the pleasure of meeting these people in person, or they were referred to me by others. As this pushed my buttons on relationship building, I started to explore networking organisations, I have to say some were simply awful, more coffee and a catch up than anything business like, but then after time I found a couple that were really proactive.

The members of the ones I enjoyed most, again shared similar values and slowly but surely I began to attract clients and build a network of people who I could count on to help my clients with services that I don't personally provide, which was simply amazing. To this day I continue to promote my business through networking, I love to build new relationships and help people.

Embracing The Victories

During our first year in business, we decided to take the biggest leap of faith we've ever taken, we sold our home and bought a smallholding in East Scotland. With the business offering a virtual service we believed it was now or never, it's certainly one of the best decisions we've made and we've not looked back. Over the past year, we've been busy setting up the smallholding and in the spring offered homes to some orphaned animals.

I find the animals a true inspiration. On the darkest of days, they lighten my life and are truly the sweetest of souls. I've recently started to write children's novels about animals, as I want to share their magic. This again is totally out of my comfort zone, something I never thought possible but I've stayed true to myself and it's really happening, with my first book due out in Autumn 2024.

One of the best things I learnt throughout life is resilience. It's been really hard at times and there will always be highs and lows in life and in business, but with sheer grit and determination, I urge you to hold your dreams tight and follow your light within.

Always stay true to yourself and trust your heart, don't let that voice in your head take over, if you believe, you really can achieve. I'm certainly proof of that!

About Me

Hi, I'm Laura Meredith, I was born in the Midlands but have recently followed my heart and moved to East Scotland and am now the proud owner of a little smallholding there. Throughout my career I've always worked for small-medium sized business providing executive assistant and bookkeeping services.

In 2021 I set up Ryedaura with my husband to offer these services to clients, we are striving to provide an exemplary service for them and a great place to work for our team. My future goal is to provide free holidays on the farm to families who have a parent poorly with cancer, to give them a safe place to relax, unwind and be amongst nature.

I'm currently in the process of writing a series of children's books to share the magic of the animals with all, and wanted to be included in this QIB book about resilience to show that if you believe you truly can achieve.

I'd like to take this opportunity to acknowledge my husband and son, for without their belief in me, this would not have been possible and to dedicate my chapter to my parents, for without their guidance I would not be the person I am today.

Face It Till You Make It

Marcela Onyx
International Best-Selling Author, Speaker, Award Winning Love And Transformational Healer & Founder
Marcela Onyx Ltd

"May we elevate our vibrations, focus on our intentions, and broaden our consciousness to truly embrace our paths."
– Marcela Onyx

Fearlessly confront challenges, recognizing them as pathways to personal growth.
Acknowledge your strengths and weaknesses, embracing authenticity throughout your journey.
Cultivate resilience by facing obstacles with a positive and unwavering mindset.
Explore every experience, understanding that each moment contributes to your continual development.

Immerse yourself in challenges, even when uncertainty limits your confidence; let authenticity guide you.
True, authentic self will help you face whatever may be holding you back, so be wise and courageous.

Take deliberate steps forward, acknowledging that progress is an ongoing journey.
Inspire yourself and others by fostering a positive attitude in the face of adversity.
Learn from setbacks, using them as valuable lessons to fuel future success.
Lead with determination, remaining committed to your goals and aspirations.

Yearn for self-improvement, - recognising the transformative power of personal growth in your life.
Overcome challenges with optimism, firmly believing in your ability to navigate through difficulties.
Unleash your potential by understanding and harnessing your unique strengths.

Make every moment count, allowing each experience to contribute to your enduring resilience.
Adapt to change with a positive mindset, finding strength in flexibility.
Keep moving forward, understanding that persistence is the key to realizing your dreams.
Embody resilience and determination, ensuring that you persist until you make it.

Illuminate your path with inner wisdom, acknowledging that self-awareness guides your journey.
Take intentional steps forward, recognizing that progress is an unending journey.

Today, I can share these wise pieces of advice, and I wonder how my life would have been totally different if I had been taught these lessons at school when I lived in Rio de Janeiro, Brazil, my native country or perhaps even when I started to work.

I still remember so clearly when I had my prom night at the age of fifteen, a magical evening where we had a wonderful ceremony followed by an unforgettable party and a conversation between my dad and one of my uncles who was retiring from the Navy. He made him a business proposition, asking him to open and manage with me what would be one of our first family shops. Come on, I was only fifteen. I had so many things that I was trying to figure out for myself at that age, and it sounded like Dad had everything planned for me. So, without having choices when the time arrived, I joined my uncle in this venture, and I must admit, I learnt a lot from the experience, it was in that commercial environment that I also met my first boyfriend, who was also running a family business and by the way, he still has his own businesses and a friendship relationship with my family.

A couple of years passed, the business was trading well, and we even managed to buy our second store. However, on the evening of 16th January 2000, we received a phone call in the middle of the night saying there had been a fire incident at the shopping centre and many stores were being affected. We quickly got changed and drove to the shopping centre, not knowing what we could expect to find, as they had not provided any information if our stores were part of the areas where the fire was; apparently, it started around 9 pm. It was a time when we had no technology as we have nowadays that usually, we can find any incident information in real-time. When we arrived there, I could see one of our stores in flames.

As a young adult, witnessing the dream of my family and the place where I initiated my career go up in flames felt like a colossal nightmare—one that you anticipate waking up from until you realise that it's damn real and devastating.

To see my family business suddenly turn to ashes was a traumatic and terrifying experience that certainly changed my life. In my perception, this story is one of a few that somehow made me feel like I had lost everything. I had to learn to find myself, gather strength to build resilience, reinvent, and find ways to start life from scratch. In this case, from ashes. I had to find a way to thrive once again.

The fire was controlled around 11 am, and a period of investigation and uncertainty started for all of us entrepreneurs who owned one or more of the 378 stores that were affected by the incident. Even though some entrepreneurs had some sort of insurance, the reality is that it took years for things to be rebuilt and for people to feel some sort of normality and certainty. Many were unable to return, and some managed to receive a percentage from insurance companies only if they had presented a copy of their invoice proving the value of their most recent purchase before the incident.

As you can imagine, back then, there were no clouds where documents could be saved online, so not much could be claimed.

Eventually, we restarted on a very small scale, and with time and perseverance, we successfully got back on track. However, the truth is, I was young and had so much to learn, away from my parents' vision and a somewhat controlling environment. I also - realised that I am someone who needs variety. I had to experience the external world. So, I started studying for a BSc in Business and Management at the University and decided to leave my comfort zone—my family business.

I realised that, by that time, with all that had happened in the past, I had developed a belief that I could be really good at making money for others. Sleeping well and enjoying my life without having to worry if, at the end of the month, we would have enough money to pay all the invoices from so many different suppliers and the staff, as the daughter of my own boss.

I started working for a company in the maritime and naval sector, with which I still maintain a great relationship, including my first boss, who became a great friend for life. I also gained experience working in the oil and gas sector, which was quite challenging in terms of management, especially regarding gender equality and diversity. One sentence that I never forgot from one of the line managers was, "Those who can command give orders, and those who are wise obey."

Embracing The Valuable Teachings

With time, I understood more about what I value in a company, my values, and why I would choose or not to work for one. I then moved on to experience working in the banking and then the fashion sector, which I really loved. Again, I still have meaningful relationships with every boss who has crossed my professional path in Brazil, where I had a successful career, money, close friends, and a loving family—all of which I'm proud of.

However, I was single for five years and longed for someone deserving of my love until I met my soulmate. This is an unusual and long story that certainly will turn into a book and would make an interesting movie. It was less than three months after his first wife (my boy's birth Mum) passed away in March 2008. When we met in person, it felt like an amazing and exciting honeymoon—an experience we never had again after getting married. Everything was perfect as we travelled to incredible destinations and spent time with my best friends; and he met my entire family and fell in love with the culture and the food.

A month later, following an eleven-hour flight, I woke up in England, embracing my soulmate's family with unconditional love and strength. I transitioned from a successful, career-driven person to suddenly becoming a mum and partner, living together right away. Sometimes, we must trust the universe's amazing and, at times, painful way of introducing turning points into our lives.

As a child adopted by my Godmother at six months old, I learned from her, my mum, that a mother is the one who raises us. I've raised my two sons with so much love and dedication since they were toddlers, and I'm grateful for the love that unites us. They are now turning into amazing adults, and both have a passion for serving, just like me.

Where my marriage is concerned, our soulmate story encountered challenges that made us stronger in our over twelve-year relationship. Like most couples, we faced moments when giving up seemed tempting, but we never did. We learned to cultivate the ability to learn and grow from experiences, to have effective heart-to-heart conversations, to be more understanding about each other's past pain and trauma, and to stop trying to change each other, building resilience and an even more meaningful connection. We realised that we were a team, and that unconditional love is non-judgmental, supportive and transformational.

Much like navigating the ups and downs of a lasting relationship, managing a successful company or investment demands similar resilience and commitment. In the corporate world, challenges are inevitable, and at times, the allure of giving up may be tempting. However, drawing from the lessons learned in enduring relationships, we recognise the importance of cultivating a learning culture. Our approach involves embracing both successes and setbacks, fostering an environment where open and honest communication is valued. Just as effective heart-to-heart conversations strengthen personal connections, transparent communication within the organisation builds trust and unity. Understanding and empathy are key as we navigate diverse perspectives, much like how a couple learns to be more understanding about each other's past pain and trauma.

In the business context, respecting diversity becomes a driving force, contributing to innovation and adaptability. Much like the realisation in a relationship that trying to change one another is counterproductive, successful companies avoid unnecessary changes and find balance in their strategies. By building a non-judgmental and supportive work environment, akin to the concept of unconditional love, we create a resilient organisational culture that encourages creativity, risk-taking, and a long-term vision.

In essence, just as a couple discovers they are a team in the face of challenges, businesses, too, understand the power of unity and unwavering commitment to overarching goals. We had different career aspirations. He worked in the IT sector for a bank, had his own businesses, and was starting his path as a football agent, while I was also exploring many paths in the personal and spiritual development field while still conciliating my role as a mother, wife and working for a Local Enterprise Partnership in the corporate world, successfully managing and over delivering projects partly funded by the European Regional Development Fund, that contributed to safeguard and create thousands of jobs while providing business support to businesses that were also contributing with the growth of the economy in the UK.

For years, I thought that I was really maximising my potential. After all, I got great recognition for my achievements and momentary happiness from breaking limits and pushing white-collar boundaries. I thought I was doing enough until it was no longer enough.

Unexpected Turn Of Events

I realised that over a decade, I had invested and gained so much knowledge and practical experience in personal and spiritual development, including, for example, five Master Teacher certifications in five different Reiki Modalities, Pure Energy Healing, and more. I felt that it was time to fully dedicate my time to my passion for supporting individuals who wanted to invest in their growth. However, life once again introduced another turning point that would forever change me and my life.

In August 2020, during the pandemic and lockdown, my soulmate suddenly and unexpectedly transitioned to the spirit world after a heart attack, leaving me in a deep pit of sorrow and grief that almost consumed me whole. The knowledge that I had did not serve any purpose because I completely lost connection with myself, my inner and external world. A huge sense of powerlessness consumed me. From my own experience, I can say that knowledge is only power when we choose to act and make the most of our wisdom through self-empowerment.

The love I received from my boys and so many people who know me worldwide touched my heart. I heard many say similar things to me, like, "You are the strongest and most determined person I know. I may not know your pain, but I know if there is someone who can overcome this situation, it's you," or "You have done so much for so many, and this is probably one of the times when others can give you some of the love and healing back that you always shared with others, so please accept our support."

The truth is, no one was able to empower me while I was disconnected from life. As a therapist and a human being, I found myself on the other side, experiencing anxiety, panic attacks, and dealing with unexpected toxic relationships. In that challenging period, I had to make the conscious decision to sit with my grief, take small steps into the healing journey and have the courage to reconnect. I needed to find inner love, peace, and rediscover my essence. With time, I empowered myself and underwent a transformation.

Healing from trauma involves recognising and managing its impact. Trauma can take many different forms, such as the failure to meet basic human needs, physical or emotional abuse, natural disasters, the loss of a job, or other life-altering events. It can cause profound changes in our lives and often leads to grief because it forces us to confront loss and change in a profound way. Even if the traumatic experience itself does not involve loss, the aftermath can create a sense of grief because we are left to process the changes that have occurred. Therefore, grief and trauma are often intertwined, and it's essential to acknowledge and address both in order to heal and move forward.

To promote healing, it's crucial to develop qualities such as patience, resilience, openness to new perspectives, and a willingness to confront difficult emotions. Additionally, prioritising self-care, setting healthy boundaries, showing kindness and compassion to ourselves, seeking support from others when needed, practising acceptance and forgiveness, engaging in creative self-expression, and recognising that healing takes time and a willingness to work through challenging experiences are essential steps.

In my case, I had to learn how to face and process the new reality that my children and I were experiencing. Despite being an evidential spiritual medium, I struggled to cope with the unexpected and unfair challenges we faced at the beginning. But I don't feel ashamed to admit that. I knew I had to find ways to reconnect with my inner power and strength to overcome the trauma, grief, and uncertainty that were taking a toll on me. Despite feeling adrift and without my supportive family roots nearby, I had to find ways to reconnect with my inner power and tap into my resilience, inner wisdom, and courage.

As I began my journey of reawakening and healing from the inside out, I started gaining clarity. I realised that, before I could once again embrace my purpose with honesty and integrity and fully serve others in their healing journey, I needed to confront my own emotional limitations, pain, and insecurities. My heart had to be filled with enough love to remember my 'why,' my purpose, and my passion for helping people heal, connect with their inner world, and develop their personal and spiritual paths.

I went through a process of self-care, self-love, self-discovery, and self-intimacy to aid my identity quest. This process helped me reconnect with my soul, rediscover old and new passions, and establish a routine that felt fulfilling. Through this journey, my life experiences, and my skills in personal and spiritual development, I delved deep within myself, reconnecting with my inner wisdom and falling in love with myself once more. This reawakened my zest for life, inner peace, and personal power.

As part of my journey of growth and self-discovery, I boldly decided to invest in myself and work with a doctor and sex coach who supported me on my healing journey. I was able to connect with my inner self as a woman and rediscover my true passions and desires. Additionally, I was inspired by another amazing doctor who shared a similar story and mission. With determination and dedication, I accomplished my assignments and exams and am now a proud certified Relationship, Intimacy, and Love Coach, as well as an International certified Sexologist.

Then, I studied to be a Medical Intuitive. It was an intense six months of my life during which I had to go even deeper to reassess my whole life, revisiting all of my past traumas. I wrote over two hundred different assignments and completed months of training and case studies. My life experiences and transformative journey, combined with my previous knowledge, have empowered me to connect with the power of love in a way that I never experienced before. This profound connection has led me to the path of becoming a love and transformational healer, driven by a genuine desire to help others understand and heal their past pain and traumas, find inner peace, ignite love, and embrace their lives and relationships with confidence and joy.

Insights Forged Through Life's Trials

Having the courage to look within and confront our past is a transformative journey that can lead to profound personal growth and healing. It's an act of self-compassion and empowerment, a decision to no longer be held hostage by our past experiences, but to instead embrace them as opportunities for growth.

To gain self-knowledge, all we need to do is look within ourselves by turning our attention inward and listening to our inner voice. Practice self-reflection, journaling, introspection, and self-analysis, and embrace who you are and who you are becoming at your core.

In the journey of self-discovery and personal empowerment, incorporating a set of principles can guide individuals towards a successful and fulfilling life, much like cultivating a successful relationship or business.

Having clarity about your goals and aspirations provides a roadmap for your personal and professional journey. Knowing your "why" – the deeper purpose driving your actions – adds meaning to your endeavours, acting as a foundation in both your personal and business pursuits. Being authentic is fundamental to genuine relationships and successful ventures. Just as authenticity fosters trust in personal connections, it forms the basis of a strong and credible brand in the business world. Recognising your strengths and weaknesses, much like understanding your partner's attributes, allows you to leverage your capabilities and address areas for improvement.

Comparing yourself to who you were yesterday, an effective practice in personal growth, mirrors the need for businesses to evolve and adapt. Seeing opportunities, providing value, and focusing on impact are crucial in both personal and professional spheres. Just as solving problems is a key element in navigating challenges within a relationship, it is equally vital in business to address issues and innovate.

Taking initiative and embracing change are qualities that drive personal and professional growth. Persisting in the face of challenges is like the determination needed to overcome obstacles in both areas. Just as individuals work on self-improvement, businesses must continuously adapt and adjust to remain relevant in a dynamic environment.

Setting high standards, handling rejection with resilience, and embracing courage are universal principles that foster success in any endeavour. Using fear as motivation, empowering oneself, and maintaining a positive outlook are transformative practices applicable to both personal and business realms. Approaching life joyously and having fun, much like cultivating a positive company culture, contributes to a fulfilling existence.

Loving oneself and taking responsibility for one's actions are foundational in personal development and business ethics. Eliminating weak speech, telling the truth, and reflecting on actions lead to authenticity and trust in both relationships and businesses. Learning from mistakes, asking good questions, and paying attention to details contribute to continuous improvement in all aspects of life.

Maintaining momentum, adjusting when needed, and cultivating successful thinking are strategies that individuals and businesses alike use to stay competitive. Believing in your abilities, exuding confidence, and becoming unstoppable are attitudes that propel personal and professional success.

Creating a schedule and valuing customers are practices that ensure organisation and customer satisfaction, respectively, in both personal and business contexts. Progressing with joy in personal growth mirrors the pursuit of happiness and fulfilment in professional endeavours.

In essence, these principles serve as a guide for individuals seeking a successful relationship with themselves and their businesses. Whether navigating personal growth or steering a company, these tips offer a holistic approach to achieving fulfilment, success, and resilience in the face of life's challenges.

Success is not just about achieving professional goals or gaining public recognition. It's about living a fulfilling life where I am healthy, empowered, and prosperous in every aspect of my being. It means having strong relationships and finding joy in the little things that bring meaning to my life. This definition of success inspires me to prioritise my well-being, nurture my personal growth, and find balance in all areas of my life. I am motivated to embrace my unique journey and to create a life that is authentically mine.

About Me

As a catalyst for transformation, Marcela's approach is grounded in a deep understanding of the complexities of human emotions and experiences. She works unwaveringly to help people overcome blockages, pain, suffering, trauma, and toxic relationships. Through this process, individuals can realign with their life's purpose, manifest their desires, and evolve spiritually, resulting in a profound transformation in their relationships, intimacy, and overall zest for life.

Marcela is a Love and Relationship Coach, recognised by the American Board of Sexology as a Sexologist, Medical Intuitive, Skilled Helper, and a qualified professional practitioner in Cognitive Behavioural Therapy, Counselling Skills, Mindfulness, and Neuro-Linguistic Programming. She is also a Spiritual Medium, Artist, Holistic Therapist, and Teacher. Marcela has a natural talent for sharing her knowledge and wisdom in powerful and captivating ways.

Guided by love, integrity, compassion, growth, and service, she is committed to authentic relationships, creativity, and resilience. With a strong foundation in Business Management and a diverse career spanning sectors like Banking, Maritime, Oil & Gas, Fashion, and Government, she merges corporate insights with transformative healing. Marcela focuses on guiding individuals through self-discovery and empowerment.

Covering various aspects such as personal growth coaching, navigating challenges (such as overcoming whistle-blowing), stress management, building resilience, improving communication skills, addressing limiting beliefs and self-sabotage, resolving conflicts, fostering effective team dynamics, cultivating authentic leadership, promoting mindfulness and well-being, boosting confidence and assertiveness, adapting to change and uncertainty, enhancing creativity and innovation, honing intuition and decision-making skills, balancing work-life and personal life, refining public speaking and presentation skills, leading with empathy and compassion, managing energy, preventing burnout, aligning business values with personal principles, and strengthening resilience in leadership, Marcela transforms challenges into opportunities.

Beyond The Shadows

Jivan Dempsey
Author, Director, HR
FiveRivers Consulting

"I can be changed by what happens to me. But I refuse to be reduced by it." – Maya Angelou

They say youth is wasted on the young.

I think they're right. It's probably unfair but I can understand why people say it. When you're young you don't know how to respond in bad situations. When you're young you don't know the right words nor behave in a way that, when you look back as your older self, you wonder what the hell you were doing? How could you be that stupid? How did you miss the signs? And weren't they obvious?

No, they weren't. When you're young, life is full of lessons that you'll come across and have to learn. Usually the hard way.

Now when I look back at my twenty-four year old younger self, one of the hardest lessons I had to learn was to understand that my words and behaviours need to be congruent. Otherwise, there will be consequences. As the memory of that time comes into focus, I'm cringing with shame and disgust. I want to push it away and most of the time I can. In my mind I'm telling myself, "If you don't think about it, it didn't happen."

But it did.

And the rise of the Me Too movement has made it virtually impossible for me to ignore and, despite my strong reluctance, forced me to look again at what happened. How did the decisions I made in that moment change my life? Why do they haunt me and what did I learn?

It's hard for me to share this memory with you as I've suppressed it for so many years. It's in a box – with the lid tightly shut – buried in a hole in the ground. Does it help? Of course not but somehow my younger self feels safer. And now with Chloe asking me to write my story I have to dig it up and look at it squarely in the face. The same way I looked at my then boss over 25 years ago, at that conference, in that hotel room as he tried to kiss me. As his attitude changed, from benevolence to maleficence when I pushed him away. As he pushed my severance letter towards me and shut the door on the job I had loved. As he introduced an attractive replacement to the team. As he put his arm around her shoulders and I realised uncomfortably, he wouldn't change and despite everything I would remain silent.

Over the many years that followed, my understanding of grooming and sexual exploitation has become clearer. What I still can't understand was, why me?

The Weight Of Regret

Back in 1993, I was very young, recently graduated and in love. When I was offered a role as HR Manager for a global pharmaceutical firm, I was so proud of myself and super excited. My life ramped up to a new level and I had suddenly become a yuppie! My salary doubled overnight and Peter, my boyfriend, and I could afford a mortgage and bought a trendy flat as our first home together. I was given a company car and ordered a red "hot hatch" which I adored racing around the country lanes. I got to travel around the world with my job, business class on both planes and trains - all the way! Yep. I was a lucky woman indeed.

I also had the best boss in the world. Ben, the HR Director, was kind and nurturing and took me under his wing. I had a lot to learn about HR, the pharmaceutical industry, and the business I was responsible for. I would be managing the HR issues associated with a specialised sales and clinical team working with the primary care sector. I was helping to grow the team, support their learning and ensure their competence and sales efforts to meet their targets. And if these targets weren't met, being ruthless to let employees go. It was a cycle. I would work closely with the sales managers, joining their meetings and providing a HR service to meet their objectives.

I loved it. I loved the work and loved the people I worked with.

Every month there were sales meetings. These one day events would be an opportunity to discuss how things were going and agree actions. Every quarter there would be sales conferences. These two day events would be to gather the sales teams to meet, learn, bond, and get a motivation boost. Every year there would be an annual conference where the sales and clinical teams would get together for three or four days at a swanky hotel to discuss corporate objectives and celebrate success. These could however become quite bawdy affairs with lots of drinking, partying and occasional bad behaviour.

I knew Ben had a thing for me. I would catch him looking at me but as he was an older man and married and I was in a happy relationship, I ignored his furtive glances and occasional flirtatious comments and focused on my work. Ben would often meet his Irish counterpart, Murray who would fly in for meetings on a regular basis. He would stay in a hotel nearby and they would meet for dinner. Sometimes I would be asked to join them. It was obvious they were pals as they enjoyed each other's company and, as they were both snooker fans, would often tour the UK and Europe together for matches.

One day Ben asked me a strange request. He said that if Murray asked me if he and I had been intimate would I say yes? I was confused. Why? He told me it was a game, not to worry about it and it was nothing serious. I was uncomfortable with this request because it was untrue. He pleaded with me and I could see a look of desperation in his face. I wasn't happy but agreed reluctantly .

Murray didn't ask me the question outright. But I could tell over the coming days and their giggling together that they had discussed it. Murray started to look at me strangely. He smiled a lot more at me, would stand too close and I felt there was a level of familiarity when he spoke to me. I was very uncomfortable around Murray as I didn't feel respected so I tried to avoid his company as much as possible. I moved towards my other HR and sales colleagues so I could work closer with them but I couldn't shake off these feelings of unease. Things felt different. Did they know? I felt dirty and deeply regretted agreeing to Ben's request. Even today I'm still angry at myself. How could I have been so stupid?

We never spoke about his request but I felt a shift in the relationship between us. He would often place his hand on my arm or the small of my back. I would sense him standing close to me, in my personal space and I would have to step away to make room. Sometimes he would run his finger over my shoulders and occasionally in my hair. It was really uncomfortable and especially so when I got an outstanding appraisal result and a big pay rise that year. I had linked these two things together rather than appreciating that the appraisal and pay rise actually reflected that I was really rather good at my job.

I dreaded our weekly one to one meetings. Back then Ben had his own office and he and I would be in the office alone for at least an hour. Before all this we worked well together. Our meetings would be fairly relaxed and easy. He was amenable and demonstrated paternal care towards me and now it was gone. I should have told Ben not to touch me, not to stand close to me, but I couldn't say the words. Why not? It was a different time. Maybe he would think I was being rude and ungrateful. Perhaps even melodramatic. He had power and I didn't, and I found myself gradually accepting the *abuse*. And that's exactly what it was. He abused his power and I was being groomed. I was angry all the time but not with him, with myself. How could I have been so stupid?

Searching For Fulfilment

I've always been an ugly duckling. As a teenager, with my brown NHS glasses, spots and platted greasy hair, I was bullied and laughed at by the girls and invisible to the boys. I was a nerd and spent my school days working hard earning my future place at university. It was my escape to be who I wanted to be, build a career and a life different to that of my parents. I saw how my parents worked so hard all their lives, in jobs they hated, sucking up to bosses who would laugh at them and abuse their position to extract gifts and money just so my parents could keep their jobs. At the time I was too young to understand but immigrant families like ours had to work harder than their white counterparts to keep their jobs and to earn a wage to provide for their children, a roof and food for the table.

The 1970s was a time of industrial change, strikes and transitioning from old heavy industries to service industries. It was the time of the National Front, rioting and racist marches through many city centres. Families like mine had to adapt. Many found themselves singled out, out of work and on the dole. Not my mum and dad. They would do anything to keep their wages coming in, which included keeping quiet about the "gifts" and bribes they had to pay. When I asked them about it they would shrug their shoulders and say we do what needs to be done. It will be different for you so don't rock the boat.

And they were right, for a while anyway. University gave me a springboard to a career that gave me hope and had so much promise. As I got older, I became more confident and started to attract attention. I've never been beautiful but pretty, with clear skin, big brown eyes and a full mouth. I liked the attention and when I met Peter I especially liked becoming a significant part of his life. Yes, life was great. Until Ben. So why didn't I speak out? I didn't want to rock the boat.

I began to question my working relationships with the other managers. What did they think of me? Did they know? I was desperately unhappy and so wanted to go back in time so I could make different choices.

A few months later there was a company announcement that the firm was merging with another pharmaceutical company. It was a great commercial opportunity, taking advantage of complementary medical products and consolidating a market position. Ben was moved to another part of the business to fulfil a different HR role. I was so relieved. He was now far away from me.

I had a new boss, Chris who took over as HR Director. He had a long career in sales and had been the Sales Director within the other organisation. We very quickly established a rapport and a good working relationship or so I thought at the time. My confidence started to return. As I was building relationships with the new sales managers and sales representatives, I started to hear things about Chris. He had a reputation as a "player" and liked blondes.

Now you're right in thinking, Jivan, how stupid are you? Yes, the man had a reputation but as I'm not blond, I didn't think it meant me.

Chris would attend all the sales meetings and conferences. He was at home in the sales world, schmoozing with sales managers and leaving me to manage the HR work. This was fine with me. I didn't really mind, and I was happy to be away from Ben. I did notice that Chris was sometimes over familiar with me, but I shrugged that off. Chris was a natural salesperson and that was just part of his sales charm. Or was it? I was keen to show Chris I was a good and capable worker and I ignored the signs. Until that is, the next annual conference and the first since the merger.

I remember a lot of bubbly, not a lot of food and having a good time laughing, drinking, and dancing. I don't remember how one moment I was talking to Chris in the conference room and the next he was with me in my room trying to kiss me. This is Chris, my new boss, crossing a line, and even in my drunken state I know what a boss is and is not meant to do. I pushed him away. No. This is not what I want. I remember my voice was feeble. He came towards me again grabbing at my shoulders and I wobbled. No. Stronger this time. I pushed at him again and somehow regained my balance. This is not what I want. I went to the bed and sat down. I was feeling dizzy, and I remember sweating. Was that in disgust, shame or both? I wanted to throw up.

My thoughts turned to why is this happening? I'm not blonde. What did I say? What did I do? Why would Chris think this was okay? He stepped back from me and our eyes locked. I saw his face change. He quickly adjusted his clothing, turned, and walked out of the room. He didn't say a word.

I ran to the door and locked it. I was so relieved, and, in that moment, started to cry. I kept replaying what had happened in my head. What had I said? What did I do? How did I end up in this situation?

I didn't know it at the time, but my life was about to change and for the worse. Here I was blaming myself and yet, as I discovered a few months later, I apparently had a reputation. Chris had heard about me and Ben from Murray and he took my rejection of him badly. But was that any excuse to take advantage? Of course not. He was embarrassed and, as I found out over the next 12 months, he wanted me out of the business.

Chris was vicious and vindictive. He made working with him a living nightmare. He wouldn't look me in the eyes. He wouldn't speak to me. He cancelled all our face-to-face meetings and would instead send me emails with his instructions and wanted reports of what I was doing. In team meetings he would single me out to tell everyone how unhappy he was with the quality of my work. He would set me tasks that were impossible and then, very often halfway through, change his mind, move the goalposts, or move the work to someone else or credit other people with the work I had done. When I tried to talk to him, he would cancel my meetings at the last minute.

Chris made this very public, and I soon found myself isolated. The sales managers were told to talk to Chris directly and I found my work being given to other HR colleagues in other parts of the business having been told I wasn't able to cope nor was I delivering quality work. My position in a few months became untenable. I know Chris wanted me to resign but I wouldn't. He wouldn't speak to me and I dug in deeper. I know I was deeply unhappy and cried a lot but I wouldn't resign. I refused to accept that the job I had loved was slowly being taken away from me. I refused to give in. And yet I was ignored, overlooked, maligned but I refused to play along with his mind games. I was so deeply unhappy. I couldn't sleep, I couldn't eat, my hair started to fall out and I became depressed. Every day I went into the office. But I wouldn't resign.

I remember a lovely spring morning. The sky was a vivid blue and the clouds were cotton wool white and so fluffy. I also remember that day for another reason. Chris came to see me. He had a letter in his hand. I looked up briefly and lowered my head when I realised it was him. We hadn't spoken for months so I didn't greet him. He pushed the letter across the desk towards me and said he wanted my decision next week. His first words to me for months since that fateful conference. There it was. My severance letter. I picked it up, read it quickly and walked out.

Paying The Price

Mine isn't a unique story. There have been many, many women in a similar position tolerating a toxic environment for their career or their family's sake. I expect most of these women, as the Me Too movement has shown, felt they had no other choice but to acquiesce, such was their fear and the level of grooming they've experienced. It's probably always been this way; since I reckon women entered the workforce - men abusing their positions to manipulate their female colleagues for their own amusement. Some women probably did what they needed to do and some would have resisted and some, like me, may have paid a heavy price.

You can't blame them. Every woman will have had to make her own choice but whatever her decision, it will leave a mark, the trauma and shock, to be carried for many years. I'm no different; the shock of realising that I was being groomed and the trauma that followed when I rejected Chris, costing me a job I loved, my reputation and my peace of mind.

I never told Pete what happened. Instead I chose to hide how I was feeling and how miserable I was. I was terrified of what he would do. Why would I want to run the risk of him ripping Chris apart? As much as that image made me smile, I didn't want to get Peter into any trouble. Instead I confided in his mum, Maureen. It turned out she herself had experienced something similar. She was a young attractive single mother and, back in 1975, that seemed to give certain men the warped idea that somehow she was "available". Her boss, a married man who was much older than her, took rejection hard. He would sit in his car outside her home watching her at all hours of the night. He insisted she work closely with him in the office. He started to follow her on weekends. This stalking went on for weeks. It terrified her and feared for her and of Peter's safety. She asked him to stop. He didn't. So she complained to another boss, again another man, and despite everything it was Maureen that was moved out of the department and shortly after dismissed from her job for poor performance. Her other boss had smeared her good reputation and character and basically lied to save his own skin. Or perhaps it was boys sticking up for each other? Maureen had loved that job. The work, the salary, the perks gone in a heartbeat because she had refused the advances of her boss and he had abused his position and had the power to basically remove her.

Maureen moved on quickly. She was able to find another job and put the unpleasantness behind her. Me, on the other hand, couldn't move on and despite finding another HR role very quickly realised I had lost more than just a job that I loved. I had lost my innocence.

The new job was good. It had a better salary and great prospects, but I struggled to fit in with my colleagues and I couldn't build a trusting relationship with my boss. I seemed to be angry all the time and often came across as prickly. I carried this anger inside me for many years as I built my career through HR operational roles and onwards into HR consulting. I didn't realise that my anger was creating a driving force that would make me successful at what I did, but also hard to work with. Maybe I held onto the anger to create a protective barrier around myself so that I could never be hurt or vulnerable again. Or, as I was to discover, perhaps I was manoeuvring into a position of power so I could abuse it myself?

A few years later I was with my team at a colleague's leaving do in a bar in central London. It was a great atmosphere. There was a lot of free drink flowing, the music was loud and we were all having fun. I found myself in a conversation with a young man at the bar who seemed very withdrawn. He wasn't part of my team but someone who had come into the bar I guess attracted by the noise and revelry. I was drunk and behaving badly. "Come and dance with me," I kept saying, pulling on his arm in the direction of the dance floor. "No!" He kept pulling his arm away from me. However I wouldn't take no for an answer and impulsively gave him a kiss on his cheek. He looked at me in shock and disgust. "That's sexual assault!" He stood up and pointed at me, shouting, "I could have you arrested!" I was taken aback. What? How was he conflating an innocent peck on the cheek to a sexual assault? Times have changed. There was no such thing as an innocent peck on the cheek, like there is no such thing as an innocent slap on the bottom, or an innocent wolf whistle. I had crossed a line when I pulled on his arm, wouldn't take no for an answer and certainly when I gave him a kiss without his permission. He was right. I was no different to Ben or Chris. As the realisation dawned on me my insides felt they were opening up and I wanted to be sick. I had repeated the pattern of abuse, a legacy from my own experience, on that young man. I was deeply ashamed and scared of what I had done.

I went home. The memory resurfaced and waves of disgust and shame kept washing over me. Oh my god, I was just like them.

The following few weeks were awful. I started to turn my anger in on myself. I refused to go to work, I wouldn't get out of bed, I wouldn't take any calls and wouldn't speak to anyone, including Peter. He was initially confused, hurt and then angry. He was at his wits end with me. I wanted help but I also refused help. I wanted to forget. I didn't want to be like them. I didn't want to be reminded of them. I spiralled into depression and self-loathing.

But I'm also a mum of two children! What's up, mum? Why are you in bed, mum? Why don't you take us to school, mum? Why are you crying, mum? It was the love (and nagging) of my family that dragged me to a therapist to get help.

Finding New Horizons

To be honest, therapy was awful. The therapist forced me to look at that painful memory and talk about what had happened. I came to understand how none of it was my fault and to appoint blame where it should be. With them. By blaming myself I was letting them off the hook, and, in the process, destroying myself. Therapy can be long and painful and healing can be slow and incremental. But when you do the work, you start to feel lighter and brighter. It's not easy and despite everything I managed to reconcile with my younger self and gradually learned to forgive her the decisions she made. Maybe in time I might even learn to love her again.

The therapist and I locked the pain and trauma away in a box and buried it deep in a hole in the ground. Was this the right thing to do? I don't know, but it was how I learned to cope and move on. I was determined not to be defined by what had happened.

As my career has grown and prospered, I am conscious of the positions that I have had the privilege to occupy. I have held senior HR practitioner and HR change leader roles for many years. With each role comes responsibility to help and nurture other team members, to coach and guide them not for your own self-interest and gratification but to help them learn from you. You become a role model to the younger generation in the workforce.

Youth is probably wasted on the young but there are lessons in life that they have to experience in order to build self-awareness and resilience. These are the lessons that I learned. I should have challenged both Ben and Chris, called out the abuse and spoken up. Like the young man in the bar, I should have defended myself. I should not have carried the anger for so many years and sought help earlier.

Now I coach and guide other HR practitioners and HR change leaders to build consulting skills and a mindset to manage change, HR transformation and be a leader and role model in their workplace. In doing so I'm transferring my own learning, strength, experience and confidence to other practitioners. I hope to help them build a level of resilience they can use in their own organisations.

About Me

With over 20 years experience at the forefront of organisational transformation, I lead change with a passion for people, having operated as a manager, consultant and non-executive director across a diverse array of public, private and third sector organisations, both in the UK and internationally.

In all capacities, I drive business improvement with people at the heart, crafting comprehensive strategies targeting transformation objectives while embedding the capabilities and cultures required to realise successful delivery.

As a result, I am adept at negotiating change at all levels of seniority, from the boardroom to the frontline, and proven in leadership development as a coach.

For more than a decade, I have operated as an independent consultant, with a speciality in HR, finance, IT, shared services and outsourcing focused transformation and change.

In addition, I am a public speaker, raising awareness of mental health issues, in my capacity as an organisational psychologist. I have a deep interest in the psychology of change, and I shape strategies based on behaviours, leadership, shared vision, collaboration and communication, to engage hearts and minds, and deliver organisational success.

Selling Now And For The Future

Suzi Seddon
Sales Coach

"Be now or be never" – Suzi Seddon

No one is born resilient. It's definitely a skill you develop and usually whilst trying to fend off the negatives in life.

Before I started my first business (selling costume jewellery), I'd already come through a major test of resilience in my personal life. So, starting a new business just seemed the next logical step to creating a new chapter in my life. I told myself that I just had myself to rely on now. That, of course, was not true but it was what I felt at the time. I was clearly using it as a distraction and a crutch, neither of which should be reasons to start any business. However, what that situation did give me was supersonic focus and that was the one saving grace I discovered for restoring my personal resilience. If you can really focus, you can move mountains. The reason I mention this to you is because my story may resonate with you. If it does, then I urge you to take time out and reconsider your position before embarking on your entrepreneurial journey, or you too may also have to pivot further down the track.

Selling costume jewellery was a really fun business. In fact, before the jewellery business, I had worked in sales across a number of market sectors for many years and to be honest it was a move to Hong Kong with my now ex-husband that precipitated the wheels falling off my wagon. There was a lot more to that story but the bottom line was that I ended up with a hefty dose of PTSD (Post Traumatic Stress Disorder) and it took over three years before I could work again. So the jewellery business was my way of getting back in the saddle, gently, to do something entirely different that put a bit of space between me and all the chaos in my life.

However, my high achiever brain was telling me I was born for more. Much more.

I swung wildly between feeling like the world needed me and massive imposter syndrome. My resilience to my own mindset was at an all time low and I knew I had a lot of work to do on that before I could move forward.

That required quite a lot of introspection, understanding why I reacted a certain way and even watching my language; I banned myself from using the word 'I' with anything negative (I can't..., I am useless..., I don't know... etc). Why? Because this is where self-esteem and confidence gets damaged and self-belief is eroded. The word 'I' is central to your being and it is really quite fragile to this type of languaging. I had to work hard to galvanise my thoughts by recognising my achievements, my expertise and secret sauce, and in part changing some limiting beliefs that were well past their due date. I had to work on my mindset, a lot.

I reflected on that 16 year old Saturday craft shop girl I once was and the day I'd made my boss some massive, tissue paper roses and she promptly sold them! You can imagine the impact that had on me but also the effect at the end of the day when I got a big boost to my wages from the sale of my paper roses! Encouraging an enterprising spirit was a skill I was taught in that shop and now it's a skill I practise, understanding from those days how impactful it was to my future mindset of what was possible, even when you just had a handful of tissue paper to work with. It programmed my mind to see that we are all surrounded by opportunity if we look for it, especially when there's a need to create extra cash to remain resilient to the financial demands of the world.

What I also realised was that in my haste to feel in control, I hadn't done any in depth, upfront analysis of 'why' I wanted to get into the jewellery business or getting really clear about what I wanted to achieve. Operating in such an unstructured way, even with supersonic focus, was not going to cut it. This was not the way to start or build a resilient business.

It was screamingly obvious something needed to change.

So with my sensible head firmly back on my shoulders, I reflected on what gifts I had to offer the world; what others found difficult and I found easy. I have always been a deep thinker, not least a quiet achiever too, so I knew I had to start over, build on stable foundations and come from a place of knowing my genius and who I was here to serve before I could move forward again.

This initial stabilisation process, where you really dig into **why** you are starting your business, is a really key part to becoming resilient in your entrepreneurial journey, especially when selling. Sales can be unforgiving, people can be brusque and dismissive so building your resilience muscle is important and that comes from clarity and certainty about what you are doing and why.

Selling is my thing. Moreover, building and managing relationships are my thing. I am in the relationship business, not the transaction business; that's my real zone of genius. I love people and it shows. I find it easy to strike up conversations with a stranger and build rapport quickly and over time I realised that others found that really difficult to do. Today I teach principally women how to sell with confidence and ease, without feeling pushy or manipulative. It's all a matter of confidence and following a well trodden process.

Situations will arise to challenge you and guaranteed, at the most inopportune moment. I have always lived by 'don't see things as a problem, see them as an opportunity'. You must calibrate your mind for success in a world of uncertainties. Not everything will work or play for you but use the experience as a learning point, stand back, counsel the opinion of others, then move forward again.

Buried treasure exists everywhere as I discovered at 16 years old in that craft shop. It also exists in your customer list where you can absolutely mine your list for the lowest hanging fruit once you know the detail about your right fit customer and what they need and want. If you don't really know who you are selling to then your business will not be very resilient. By being resourceful and controlling growth in your business by minimising the need for marketing spend, at least in the early days, is definitely an area to start to build resilience.

But there are three other areas I'd like to focus on:

1. Resilience Built From Within

As the next generation of female entrepreneurs, I feel it's important to stress that you don't need to become someone else to be successful, you don't need to wear a mask or imitate a well-known guru… you just need to be you. Why? Because today authenticity is big. Gone are the days of the super slick salesperson. People want to feel cocooned; to live in a safe bubble with people they know, like and trust. Our world faces so many uncertainties. We all crave certainty, don't we?... in our jobs, our relationships but also in the choices we make as to how we spend our time and money wisely. When we feel certain, we feel resilient because we have dynamically linked trust to our world and all who touch it.

In sales, being trustworthy is imperative because it helps establish credibility making customers more likely to believe and invest in your product, program or service. In psychology, authenticity promotes honest communication and a foundation for great customer interaction and relationships. So we need to really be in touch with ourselves at our very core.

Luckily, women are born with a myriad of natural, feminine superpowers; warmth, empathy, conversation, listening rather than talking over someone, asking open questions, nurturing our customers, tapping into our intuition, being interested and interesting, utilising creative thinking and problem solving skills. These are our powerful assets and they are key to you unlocking your potential… if you use them!

Speaking from our centre is where we come face to face with our beliefs and values, right on the precipice with self-esteem, confidence and imposter syndrome that can feel like dancing with the devil to us. The question is how do we deal with this?

Every sales course I have ever attended was taught by a man and what occurred to me over the years was that it was a very one-sided view, probably influenced by my days in the craft shop being taught by a woman. I do believe it was this that gave me real insight into the differences between how men and women differ when selling.

A positive and energetic demeanour can influence potential customers, making them more receptive to your message. Enthusiasm is contagious and can create a real sense of excitement about your product, program or service. It builds confidence and trust, making it more likely for customers to engage and make a purchase and plays a significant role in shaping the perception of your offer and influencing buying decisions.

The energy with which you show up in front of your prospects really matters. They feed off it. The first few seconds are the moments when people subconsciously decide on their initial reaction to you. Just like magnets that can attract or repel, as humans we all do this too. So it's important to meet prospects with the same energy they display, so you can equalise and mirror them in terms of energy, tonality and body language. All of these components feed into their psyche as they weigh up whether they are going to open up to you, or shut you down!

Part of your energy will be driven by how you feel about what you are selling. Do you have full confidence in it? Do you have confidence in yourself? Do you know the facts and figures of your offer? Have you asked lots of open questions to unearth hidden information?

When you walk into a room the energy is palpable. I remember going to an Italian restaurant one New Year's Eve with my boyfriend and two friends and there was absolutely no one else in there. Obviously the atmosphere was flat and I think we all felt we'd made a huge mistake. However, five minutes to midnight about 40 Italians arrived upstairs from the undercroft (they were the extended family of the restaurant owners) and we ended up having the party to end all others well into the night. Basically, the energy had arrived. Finally we were picking up good vibrations.

Energy is fundamental to projecting enthusiasm and confidence in what you sell. Your audience has to be really sure that you are the person who holds the solution to their problem. If you look unsure or sound unsure, they won't buy. That is the simple truth.

This is not about being loud or pushy, it's about being warm, smiling and inviting. It's about listening, answering questions then asking more to open up a wider discussion so you can easily see if you have the right fit solution for what your prospect seeks. Come from your centre with clarity, confidence and certainty – that's where the magic meets the mettle.

2. Resilience In Action

Lead with Grace

Navigate challenges with composed demeanour, inspiring your team even in difficult times. Clear communication is imperative when building a team. They need to know what is expected of them so they can represent your business effectively. A team that cannot pull together does not instil confidence into prospects or long-standing customers.

Network and Empower

Cultivate a strong network, share experiences, offer support and empower each other to overcome obstacles. Resilience is strengthened through collaborative efforts. Community spirit is really important and finding others who are treading the same path will be an enormous support to you. Don't underestimate this.

Adaptability is Key

In the dynamic business landscape, being resilient means staying adaptable and flexible. Embrace change, pivot when necessary and view challenges as opportunities for growth and innovation. Your business today will probably bear little resemblance to the one you lead in 10 or even 5 years time. Technology and how we all embrace it, is speeding up the way we do business today with important and ground breaking discoveries that will impact us all.

Confidence in Decision Making

Trust your instincts and decisions. Resilience comes from the confidence to make tough choices, learn from them and continuously evolve your strategies to navigate the complexities of entrepreneurship. As children we are all very instinctually driven but with the passage of time, we all become more cautious and that directly affects how we react. Be mindful about what decisions you have made and why you made them.

Cultivate a Positive Mindset

Maintain a positive outlook, even when things don't go to plan. Cultivating resilience involves seeing setbacks as learning experiences, fostering a mindset that propels you forward despite challenges. This is especially important if you have a team around you who will look to you as the gold standard for the way things should be done, for leadership and for inspiration.

3. Resilience For Tomorrow

Resilient businesses leverage trend insights to adapt their strategies proactively. Whether it's embracing new technologies or aligning with evolving consumer preferences, staying resilient means being agile and ready to pivot when trends dictate.

Of course, trend analysis also relates to what's happening right now in your business, so you definitely need to keep an eye on what's happening in the here and now as well as looking to the future. Look at your customers' behaviour. Has it changed? Whereas once upon a time they stayed with you for 3 years, are they now leaving after 2? Why?

Resilience begins with foresight. Trend forecasting allows businesses to anticipate shifts in consumer behaviour, industry dynamics and emerging technologies. Being ahead of the curve enhances your ability to adapt swiftly to changing landscapes. Be well read. Educate yourself. Be aware of the world around you. Watch changing trends and new innovations. Future proof yourself, your skillset and your business.

Trend forecasting encourages a culture of innovation. Resilience is not just about weathering storms but thriving in them. By identifying trends, businesses can innovate and position themselves as leaders, turning challenges into opportunities. For many years, I have followed the work of Faith Popcorn; trend forecaster extraordinaire, who has been guiding the Fortune 200 companies for over 40 years. Faith and her team track trends and cultural currents and shifts worldwide through interviewing thousands of thought leaders. They analyse the data and formulate a list of trends and then predict the mood of society for the development of new products. All of these predictions are based on around 10+ years of research, enabling them to be incredibly accurate. In fact 95% accurate. 40 years ago, it was Faith's team that predicted the movement toward the vast uptake in 4 x 4 vehicles.

Many other vertical trend analysis companies exist, but more specifically in vertical markets, for example, www.wgsn.com in fabrics and www.insiderintelligence.com in marketing research.

Trends often follow patterns. A resilient business learns from past trends and disruptions, using historical data to build strategies that are not just reactive but proactive in navigating future uncertainties. In essence, combining trend forecasting with resilience equips businesses to not only survive but thrive in an ever-changing market. It's a dynamic dance where staying one step ahead allows businesses to turn challenges into stepping stones to success.

There are companies right now developing ways of turning flood water into drinking water, developing cities for thousands of people with every amenity they want or need within 5 minutes of where they live. This is not the stuff of dreams or the far distant future, just like that song recorded by Meat Loaf alluding to "objects in the mirror may appear closer than they are". Think about innovations we know about on the near horizon like 'Apple Vision Pro', Apple's mixed reality experience headset designed to take us on journeys right from within our homes. Then consider Chloe, the first personal assistant android developed by Cyberlife who can perform the role of Receptionist or maybe even Housekeeper. Also consider the impact of having Chloe in your business. She needs no vacations, or paying, she doesn't even need the lights on to work! Imagine her role in your world today. This is all coming very, very soon as are personalised robots that will be calibrated to you, to satisfy your personal needs! Yes, I know it's shocking but it **is** on the fairly near horizon.

Resilience is fortified through diversification. Trend forecasting helps identify potential areas for diversification, spreading business interests across various trends to create a more stable and adaptable operation.

Today's Alpha generation (born 2010-2025) are beginning to describe themselves as Homo-Techno – half human, half computer. Not a surprise really when the jobs of the world right now are handled 50% by humans and 50% by machines or computers as identified by Brain Reserve's research.

The point is you need to know about this stuff if your business is going to be resilient going forward. For a moment consider things that are happening in your own world right now. Those little changes in behaviours that didn't exist a few years ago. Once upon a time people used to go out at 11pm having had a snooze and then party all night long. Now people of all ages I know are going to bed at 8pm. Restaurants are emptier in the evenings and busier at lunchtimes. If you are in hospitality what effect is this having now and more importantly what are the trends for the future? My advice is to seriously start thinking about all of this.

The world is not standing still, nor can you afford to.

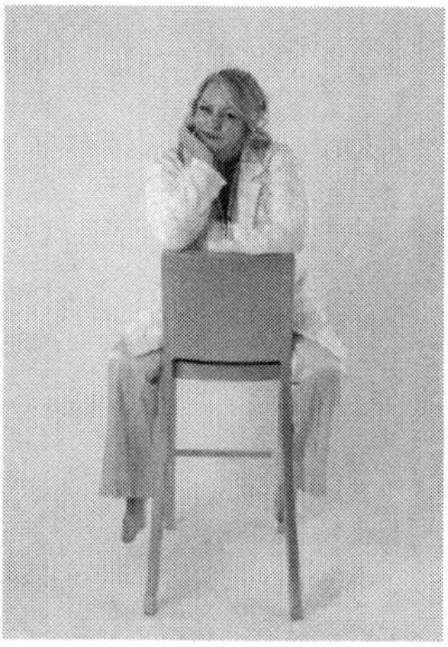

About Me

Suzi Seddon is a sales coach, bestselling co-author and thought leader with over 30 years of experience in sales. After battling the male-dominated approach to sales, Suzi created her Flow State Selling System to help women to use their feminine energy to sell without the sleaze. She's on a mission to empower female entrepreneurs to sell and win more business by embracing their feminine superpowers.

Are We There Yet?

Karen Wigley
Entrepreneur and NLP Practitioner
Promachfinish and KEW Property Rentals Ltd

"Life is either a daring adventure or nothing at all."
– Helen Keller

Do you remember as a child going on a car journey, a journey where? Did it even matter? I was always the one in the car, wondering "Are we there yet?". I remember pestering my parents with this question every time we would jump in the car. It was a red car that had faded a little, the door was heavy as I pulled on the handle, and my legs were too small just to step in, so I had to climb onto the beltless seat. I remember feeling like a proper family doing something most people would take for granted, however not many people in my area had a car. So these times were very special, my mum, dad and big brother didn't go on these trips often, and chances are we would only be on this particular journey for a short time too. But to me as a kid any time was a long time to be in the back of a car. No seatbelts, no music and wondering "Are we there yet?".

I used to think all journeys involved some vehicle, something with wheels to be driven from one destination or another, you know the A to B kind. However, it took me a very long time to realise there is more than this type of vehicle. Our body is also a vehicle, a vessel in which we travel. Our journey involves our physical body, our thoughts, desires, doubts and our dreams.

When you have a crystal clear destination and you know what you want, you can make miracles happen. When you start to get out of your own way and decide your direction in life, the world is your oyster, if that's what you want. However, the importance of clarity is not to be underestimated. This has been one of my major challenges amongst the many other lessons I've had to learn quickly as I grow with my business.

In all the decades I've travelled through my life unknowingly wasting time, just living my life unconsciously, taking everything in my stride without question. I realised I'd never been asked or even asked myself what I wanted to do with my life. I don't mean what I wanted to do for that day or weekend but what I wanted from my life. I'd convinced myself I was only worth a minimum wage, I thought my value was the lowest monetary value it could be.

Don't get me wrong I enjoyed these jobs and took great pride in every one of them, I had to endure, however, these were a means to an end. Something inside was missing and I didn't know what it was. I was under the impression I was only good for low paid service industry jobs. I was no longer asking 'Are we there yet?' and I started asking myself 'Am I there yet?'.

During my school years being a young teenager, moving countries had a major impact on my education. I started to rebel against learning and my mum for making me move from England to Scotland. My education suffered, not that I was academically bright, however I carried on regardless. I worked hard while bringing up my children on my own, always wanting better for them and never getting far. I attended college in my early twenties part-time doing mathematics and communication. Then I attended a full-time course but finished after the year so I could be home with my children.

Going from one job to another drifting through life once again. I needed to change to be a good role model for my girls. I eventually applied to university as a mature student. However, after studying for seven years to get a degree I went back to service jobs again. I had everything anybody could ever want, two beautiful children, a roof over my head and food to eat. What was this 'thing' that I was missing in my life?

Searching For My Dad

I know having a clear set goal and focusing all your energy on what you want to achieve most definitely works, I have firsthand evidence of this. My dad hadn't been in my life for around 24 years, he had been missing for more of my life than he'd been a part of it by this point. He had missed so much, so many things a dad should be around for. However, we had moved away for reasons I didn't know about and no one who stayed in my hometown had seen him in a long time. I thought he must have died.

I expected to get confirmation of this one day when I got a call from my sister asking if I'd seen the news. I hadn't. The news in my home town wasn't covered in Scotland. I had to search for the news article online to see the photofit. This was in the time of dial-up internet so I waited patiently as I looked up the story my sister had told me. The body of a man had been found in the grounds of a hospital and the police were looking for relatives to identify him. The picture of the unknown man could be my dad, the ages were similar and the location made sense. It had been so long, was this my dad? The picture on the screen came down in slow motion and bit by bit. This man's face was staring back at me and I couldn't be one hundred percent sure it was my dad.

What I did know was there was an unidentified body that needed to be identified, so the next day I called the police. I was put through to Manchester CID, they asked a lot of questions that I didn't have any answers to. At this point from this phone call, I knew I needed to find out what happened to my dad, in the hope of eliminating him from the unidentified body.

A new journey had presented itself, at this point in my life, I was a mature student with two teenage daughters in the final year of my degree. The turmoil I had overcome to get to this point of my life, especially with the crucifying self-doubt and the struggles I faced. It wasn't easy being back in education after so long away, however the passion never wavered over the years. Here I was in my final year and now facing the prospect of searching for my dad. I'd been studying for two years before to gain the qualifications needed to gain access to university, so I was not giving up now. I was so close to finishing my years of studying and changing my life for the better.

You see I was under the impression if you worked hard and gained a degree you could change your life and build a flourishing career. I needed this to create a better life for my children. I spoke to my Director of Studies the next day to talk about the possibility of taking a year out as my priorities had shifted. Ultimately he persuaded me to stay on and complete the last year, he was worried I wouldn't come back and finish the degree. Whether this was the right decision or not I took his advice and carried on with my fourth year.

Although I couldn't focus on anything, all my attention and energy was on finding my dad. I started speaking to register house in both Scotland and my home town. The fact I was trying to find my dad while I lived more than 200 miles away also didn't help, but my determination and drive kept me going. I kept coming across brick walls at every turn morning, noon and night. I was obsessed with finding out where my dad was. I was speaking with everyone that I could think of and that would listen.

It became so hard to focus on my daily duties and responsibilities. I was a volunteer at the Student Union Advice Place. My shift was every Tuesday afternoon, I had never let them down, I couldn't believe I was even considering it. My thoughts were elsewhere. I was in no position to offer people advice. I phoned The Advice Place and although I knew I was letting them down, I knew I had to make the most of this time. I had now been looking for my dad for three weeks and I was getting nowhere fast. Yet this feeling inside was telling me to keep going. So that afternoon I continued my search and for some reason, I remembered the hospital my dad used to visit regularly when I was a child. At the same time, I was thinking "Where did that thought even come from?" I was simultaneously thinking "Why didn't I remember this place sooner?". I was again on the phone with a stranger telling them my story of how I needed to find my dad.

Well, I couldn't believe it when the person on the end of the phone was saying "Yes I know your dad, do you want his address?". Was this happening so quickly, had I found my dad after all these years? Was I going to be meeting my dad after thinking I had no parents for the past 18 years - within four weeks of deciding I needed to find my dad to talk with him on the phone?... It took only four weeks! I really couldn't believe it, but it was an amazing shock to be in. I tried finding my dad in the past, but this time the energy I put into it was very different. Having a passion for something and not letting anything stop you from getting what you want, is way more powerful than you can imagine. It can feel quite unbelievable and magical when you achieve it.

What Are You Attracting

When used correctly the law of attraction is unbreakable and proves miracles can and do happen. I didn't need to know where to start on my journey of finding my dad. I just needed to have the passion and take the action required. The universe was guiding me in the right direction and putting me in touch with people who helped me along the way. I was feeling so fed up after a few weeks of getting nowhere in the search for my dad. That afternoon I took time off from my duties at The Advice Place, my energy must have shifted to remember the department he would visit regularly. I was fed up that afternoon and decided I was phoning the hospital.

Using this law as a tool in business and throughout life will certainly help when issues arise, which they inevitably will. For any business to progress you need to be constantly moving and adapting as the market changes. Being in charge of your destiny with no limits is certainly better than any job I've ever had the pleasure of experiencing. It's also allowing me the freedom to do things I hadn't even dreamed of like writing the chapter for this book. Being persistent with your goals no matter what obstacles present along the way allows your energy to flow.

Being open and looking at life differently has certainly made a huge impact on what I know can be done, therefore anyone else can do too.

It takes work, but remember when you're doing something you love can it be classed as work? I don't think so. I love absolutely everything that I do now because I've created what I wanted, I found what I'm passionate about and what makes me happy. It's taken me a lot of time and wasted energy to figure this out but now I feel able to move forward as I have a clear focus and a plan of action. However, time is non-negotiable and is your highest commodity. Therefore you need to use your time wisely, something I've not previously done and now have slight regret I didn't learn this sooner especially with the information I now have.

Life Learns And Investment

What I've realised in life is that time does go by so quickly, certainly not like the family drives as a kid. In the business world, it feels much quicker. You have to filter everything out to what is relevant as there is so much information out there, especially for people new to business like myself. My best advice is always to do your research first and just take the action to jump straight in and get started. There is never going to be a 'right time' you just need to do it and then keep working on it. Please don't waste your time like I did and regret it. Now I'm constantly on a learning curve and love everything I do.

My future is all mine, I have freedom and I now decide and make my own decisions. This was not always my reality. I just kept moving forward and searching for something that was missing in my life. That all changed when I decided to invest in my future.

In October 2021 I signed up to Steven Green Property Investment Academy (PIA), attending the three Day Advanced Training in November. This was one of the most fearful things I'd done as I never thought I would ever invest money in my learning after university. I hadn't realised how scared I would be walking into a room full of strangers on my own and not knowing what to expect or even if I was doing the right thing. I didn't need to worry as throughout my training I started to open up. The coaches were amazing and the information packed into the three-day event was life-changing. All the people were so friendly and I certainly made friends for life. This brings me nicely to one of the most highly valued aspects of business, networking.

We couldn't survive in business without a good network of people around us. When you're not a natural conversationalist, networking can be a daunting experience. However, just like anything you haven't done-before, getting out of your comfort zone shows you are progressing in the right direction. Plus the more you do it, the easier it'll become and you'll start to find yourself enjoying the experience.

The three day property course certainly started my transformational journey of why am I here? What is my true purpose in life? You know the normal stuff you get on a property course. This was the first time in my life I'd thought about mindset training that was easy to understand and implement. My first time networking with so many people, and meeting strangers who have become lifelong friends. Being part of the PIA Community opens up your network to other people all wanting the best for each other. In January 2022 Steen Green put on a free event called Strength 2 Succeed. Two full days of mental health awareness and motivational speakers each telling their inspirational stories. I mentioned it to my partner Alan, who liked the idea of it. We weren't sure what to expect over the two days, however we met people who are now friends for life. I came out of the event and walked around the back of the building to see Steven Green talking to a member of his staff. I don't know what came over me but I heard myself saying 'I'll be on Elite in March'. I certainly didn't know how I was going to do it, but remember I didn't need to.

Taking The Elite Step

Elite was in six weeks and I didn't know where I was going to find the money to pay for it. It was a lot of money to find, especially in such a short time. I just had that feeling, that same gut instinct when looking for my dad, that this was what I needed to do. I had a banking app and after I pressed a few buttons and next thing I had the money in my bank to pay for Elite. I was in… Elite 11! Seven days of intense property training, staying in a five-star hotel, on my own again. I jumped all in and found myself feeling totally out of my depth but loving every second of it. The experience from the whole week will stay with me forever.

My journey home from Elite training was surreal. Something even deeper had fired inside me. Morning, noon and night I was researching property trying to find a good deal worthy of investment, but nothing was suitable. Four weeks after I got back from Elite I woke up during the night and remembered a few years ago Armando (someone I'd previously done some work for) had offered me to rent one of his short-term holiday lets and I'd take control of everything. It was a fabulous opportunity at the time, but my mind was limited in what I thought I was capable of. Therefore, I declined the opportunity as I didn't think I could run such a business. So with my renewed mindset, I got in touch with Armando the next morning and we arranged a meeting to discuss the opportunity he'd offered me years ago. I was very lucky as he was just in the process of putting the house onto the market to sell. Instead, this was the start of my Ltd company being born in July 2022. Lots of late nights and hard work to begin with, however that's become easier as my experience has grown. More importantly, my journey of discovering why I do what I do had me constantly thinking and always wanting to learn more.

Yes of course there will be difficult times ahead, that's all part of business and life in general, but with the correct plans and strategies in place, you will become resilient and therefore grow stronger as you learn more. Adding to your life's journey and doing what you really enjoy doing. Now who doesn't want that?

Nearly There?

I heard about a Neuro Linguistic Programming (NLP) course and was interested in finding out more information. I signed up straight away to get to the practitioner level, this was to help me with the insecurities I had built up over the decades.

Having techniques to put in place when life challenges us is a very powerful tool to have at your disposal. The week-long experience where I gained my certificate and made 15 lifelong friends added so much more to my life. More importantly, I realised I had found something I loved to do, helping other people with issues, who feel lost in life and don't know where to seek help. I felt selfish keeping this knowledge to myself and knowing how I feel about self-improvement, that any of us can change if we want to. I started my NLP Practice and looked into learning more about transformational coaching. I look forward to attending the Masters level of NLP soon. The more I invest in myself the more I can give back to my clients so they can be the best they want to be.

Always Moving Forward

Taking the plunge into investing in yourself may seem alien to you as it used to feel to me. I thought only people with money could invest in themselves. People like me just go to work and carry on doing the same thing day in and day out without even thinking about what direction my life is going. This is most definitely not the case. Finding out your 'why'; what you really want to do, making a plan and taking action will open up new opportunities only if you are true to yourself. By putting yourself first and being the best you can be, you can then be the best for others in your life. What I've achieved in the past two years has been transformational and this is whether I wanted it or not. I know I couldn't carry on the life I was leading. Something had to change, and that had to be me. My beliefs were so limited I stood in my way my whole life and it was not until after my property training and my mentor mentioned this that I realised I was my saboteur.

In your journey, you will be challenged at every corner of your business. This is where the excitement is as you are constantly learning and adapting. Find out what you are passionate about, put it into something you love and your business will become a joy and a pleasure to spend time in and on. The challenges you are presented with will certainly help you grow in your new experiences. You'll then have the tools available to help others in the same position in the future. A win-win situation for everyone involved because helping others is so satisfactory.

Our life journey happens whether we take full control of it or not. Taking full control allows you to decide what you want to do. You have more potential in you than you can imagine. Getting out of your own way and pushing your boundaries will impact your life, confidence, self-esteem and what feels like miracles that happen along the way. Whatever the outcome, successful or not, lessons will have been learned. And that my dear friend is what our journey is all about, being happy in the moment and being grateful for everything we have and we cannot go far wrong.

About Me

My name is Karen and I'm new to the business world. Growing up in poverty when I was a child and bringing my children up while I was on benefits certainly had an impact on how I looked at the world. I thought this was my life and I couldn't do anything about it. However, I just kept on living my life and moving forward. Things started to develop when I started a joint vehicle scratch repair business with my partner in 2018. In the past two years, I've started a property business, gained a Neuro Linguistic Programming Practitioner level and started practising. In May 2024 I will be sitting my NLP Masters level as my passion is with helping others to help themselves. I am very privileged to have been a young mum and now a grandmother to three beautiful grandchildren.

I'm a natural introvert, I used to think there must have been something wrong with me. Finding and using my voice has been new to me in the past 18 months. I'm constantly learning and taking full control of my life, setting monthly goals. Nowadays I'm either spending time with family, working on the businesses, working out or working on my spirituality.

I want to dedicate this chapter to my two beautiful daughters who have taught me so much over the decades. They have both been pivotal in the person I have become today. Together as a family, we have endured many ups and downs but we have grown older together and still have a blossoming relationship. I feel blessed and I wouldn't have it any other way.

Legacy In Progress

Jennifer Opare-Aryee
Award Winning HR Expert, Founder of The Mary Sowah Foundation &
Founder JOA HR Consulting Limited

"No condition is permanent." – Jennifer Opare-Aryee

I was born in Ghana in West Africa, but I immigrated to the United Kingdom when I was 15 years old to join my father, stepmother, and half-siblings. My biological mother and other relatives later relocated to the UK. The UK has been my home for over three decades.

The transition of immigrating so close to my final year at secondary school affected my grades. Although I spoke fluent English when I came to the UK, the move was a life-changing event in my young adult life. I had transferred as a general arts student from an African country to a Western country and I was asked to choose G.C.S. Es subjects such as graphics and modular science that were alien to me. History, law, English language, and literature were some of my favourite subjects but the UK curriculum was completely different.

Despite that, I had good, predicted grades but additional tuition would have facilitated a smooth transition. The style of teaching and culture was new to me, my grades suffered and as a result, I went from being a great student to an average student. There is something about planning and preparing that gets you closer to achieving your goals. It is a life lesson that I have learned along the way.

My G.C.S.E grades did not deter me from furthering my education and I went on to graduate from Manchester Metropolitan University with a degree in Business Administration and a Master's degree in Human Resources. Before I embarked on my master's degree, I held jobs in HR during the summer holidays including work shadowing to get practical experience. This reinforced my resolve to pursue a career in human resources.

Before beginning university, my father and I experienced a strained relationship; he ceased communication and cut off financial support. Initially, unaware of his reasons, I felt a sense of unfairness as others verbally criticised me for alleged offences. Fortunately, my part-time job allowed me to save for university and cover transportation costs. Despite feeling isolated, our relationship improved before university, surprising my father with my independence and resilience.

My interests and hobbies extended to reading, and I credit my mother for fostering my love for it. She encouraged me to read newspapers at a young age and even read them to me.This led to a passion and interest in journalism however, I was not encouraged by career advisors when I shared my ambition with them and for a while I was lost and unsure of my career options. I had an interest in law and history and that became my fall-back plan. I had wanted to do English Language, Literature, History and Law in college but my father wanted me to do politics, he wanted at least one child to become an MP. This was far from my chosen path, and I changed direction to business studies. It was while I was in college that I was first introduced to people management which spiked my interest. I discovered that I had a natural flair for it and also covered aspects of law. I had the pleasure of meeting and talking to a kind HR director from the YMCA and her encouragement gave me the boost I needed to consider HR as a career option. It is amazing how the alteration of my career choice resulted from a surprising lack of support and encouragement from career professionals, while unexpected support from an unlikely source opened the door to a new career direction.

What I have learnt is the influential power of words and how they can significantly impact those who may seek guidance from us.

The Journey To Starting My Consulting Business

I set up JOA HR consulting business 13 years ago. The business is based in Essex but operates nationally. We provide a range of services from Employee Relations, Employee Engagement, change management, Pay structure and review and strategy development to small to medium-sized business and HR departments.

Setting up the business was a spur of the moment decision, and this came about because of taking a contracting assignment through a recruitment agency that advised me at the time to set up a limited company. Apart from the legal set-up, the business didn't have the structures to function as a business. I was working via recruitment agencies and the company was the tax-efficient way to make decent earnings. When IR35 was implemented in the public sector, I was no longer able to work under the limited company due to how I was operating as a business. Thus, the business was dormant until 2020 when I made a conscious decision to run the business full-time. The pandemic presented a barrier and further delayed my agenda.

Before setting up the business, I had worked in the corporate world in Human Resources for over 2 decades. Thus, I had the knowledge and a business degree, but I lacked the practical experience to successfully operate a business. I attended several courses in preparation for running the consulting business in 2021. Behind the scenes, the business operated as a side hustle in the interim until I completed a Leap into HR Consulting course in May 2022. Following the successful completion of the course I resigned from my job, and I have been running the business full-time since 2023.

Multiple Streams Of Income

I've always had an entrepreneurial spirit and when I started working in the corporate world, I tried to have other alternative sources of income. I dubbed in several things from selling make-up, and other business ventures to investing in properties. Indeed, I bought my first property with my part-time income from Barclays and funds from family members before I completed my studies.

You see, I have always been a hustler and a believer in multiple streams of income. I learnt this from my grandmother. She was a cook in a boarding school in Ghana until she retired. During the holidays she will have other side hustles and I have vivid memories of working with her on some of these ventures. She also advised me and others to have vocational skills in addition to formal education and learn to eat from our hands (a literal translation from my mother's tongue).

Getting a mortgage with a part-time income was not easy and I was also deterred from well-meaning estate agents to avoid buying properties in certain areas in Manchester. However, shortly after I bought my property in an undesirable location that had the presence of gang life, the UK won the bid to host the Commonwealth Games in Manchester and the area was transformed and became one of the sought-after locations due in part to its proximity to the universities, Manchester Airport, the city centre and shopping centres etc. The price of my property increased by five folds and I released the equity to buy my second and third properties in London. It was ground-breaking at the time because I was the first out of my friends and family to have bought a property before finishing university. Along the way, I had setbacks with tenants and estate agents which were challenging and stressful.

Shaping My Destiny

The drive behind my business in 2020 was to change the narrative. I was tired of waiting to be seen and for others to see my wealth. I didn't want to play the victim and allow my circumstances to determine my future. I wanted to take charge of the narrative and be in control of my career development and my work. However, the motivation changed when I made a promise to my grandmother to allow my niece in Ghana to come and live with me in the UK to study medicine. I felt having the business would allow me to balance childcare with work and provide me with the flexibility to support my niece to transition to the UK seamlessly and avoid my experience.

My grandmother died in December 2017 and my drive and motivation for the business changed to building a legacy to honour her. This led me to set up a not-for-profit organisation to remove the barriers that prevent a child from getting a basic education. I needed the consultancy business to succeed so I can have the time and the financial freedom to commit to the cause.

My Fears And Challenges

I have a curious mind and a daring nature to succeed. Thus, it is often when I am knee-deep into a project that the full weight will hit me, and imposter syndrome may set in. There was never a doubt initially that the business may struggle. I had a conviction to succeed in building a legacy that will help others break generational barriers to education; however, there have been moments in my business journey when I have questioned whether I am good enough and if I can succeed. Finding clients and having a steady flow of income is challenging for a start-up business and I have experienced dry spells that have financially incapacitated me. I had not appreciated the challenges that came from my visibility strategy and raising my authority to get more clients. I was as prepared as I could to lay a strong foundation to run my business, but it was only when my income to keep a roof over my head that some of the fears and doubts started to creep in. There was no guaranteed income at the end of the month. The plan for most of 2023 was also to increase my visibility and authority and that came with making some key decisions and taking on some courageous actions. For example, being on an American television and podcast or social media wasn't something that I wanted to do. I had the traditional view of running a business and in the past, I've had success from referrals but they were not sufficient to have a steady flow of income to operate the business full-time. I had to learn to overcome the barriers that were preventing me from being visible.

Dealing With Barriers

The best way for me to unlock and deal with barriers was for me to identify the blockages and remove them by revisiting my "why". At times there were voices from well-intended family members and friends that tried to present other options. The fears I developed halfway through my business journey were based on naivety. I had high expectations because of my referrals through networking, only to realise that I had underestimated the time commitment required before seeing a return on investment.

When the offers and referrals didn't come flooding in, I queried whether I was doing the right thing. The fear wasn't based on a dwindling income and mountain expenses and lack of consistent income. It became tempting to throw in the towel and return to the corporate world because it offers a guaranteed income. The challenge was to have a working capital to keep the business afloat. You can have a belief or hope but ultimately money is what will become a well-oiled machine that will run the business and when you have relied on family members and friends to support you financially and the well-had run dry, the fear becomes a real thing when the month is getting closer to the end and direct debits are scheduled to be debited out of your accounts and you don't know where the money is going to come from to pay your bills. It created a kind of financial stress for me that I had never experienced before.

Managing Imposter Syndrome And Setbacks

When imposter syndrome set in, I tried not to allow it to consume me. I listened to the voice, and I presented a counterargument to steer me back on course. It became incredibly difficult when I couldn't raise capital from the banks, and I had exhausted my loved ones' finances and there were a mountain of bills to be paid. The difficulty with the fears and the challenges for the business is that it spills over to the personal side. I had hoped to be in a position to launch my podcast in 2023.I had committed a lot of time to finding my niche that aligned with my values and I had lined up guests and a friend had offered his recording studio to me. Sadly, he lost a close family member and that delayed the recording. Lack of finance also meant that I couldn't book a studio to record the podcast. I also had visitors over the summer period which made my home unsuitable for the recording. I was also mindful that some of my guests live outside of London and therefore the face-to-face recording may not necessarily work. At times, it felt like one rolling barrier after the other. Therefore, I took stock over the Christmas period to re-evaluate and explore other options to achieve the same outcome.

The setbacks that I experienced were like works of art and it manifested and derailed my planned LinkedIn live events in 2023. Fast forward to 2024 and I now have three events lined up in January. The key is to never give up. One of my grandmother's pieces of advice is for God to give us a long life. A delay in a project isn't what matters but time. Long life gives you a chance to achieve your goals. As far as you have life you must never give up on your dreams however long it takes. You must also have the determination when doors are shut, or unforeseen barriers are elected to find a way to sidestep around the barriers.

Making Bold And Courageous Decisions

Despite the number of setbacks in 2023, I have enjoyed some successes. For instance, I took the bold decision to approach the Federation of Small Businesses to be a speaker. My offer was accepted and I presented in October, and I was also on the panel in November. Additionally, I was nominated for a few awards and I was a runner-up and winner for two separate awards.

My visibility plan for 2023 led me to join Queens Get Seen Accelerator course with Queens In Business, and eventually I proceeded to sign up to their PR agency, which is the Queens Media Agency. To onlookers, it may seem like a smooth transition, but it was a balancing act to raise the capital to invest in the business when resources were already stretched, and clients were non-existent. I sacrificed where I could, and the benefits yielded dividends in articles publications and award nominations. My visibility grew both in the UK and the US.

I also faced my fears and did a Facebook live and I have been a guest on several podcasts and have had a few articles published. Some of the activities were outside my comfort zone but I took a courageous decision to challenge myself. We can do incredible things far beyond our expectations if we give ourselves the space to be courageous. For me, my way of overcoming fear is to have the audacity to dare to hope and that becomes greater than my fear and setbacks. Indeed, I was once told I was like the dog that would not let go of the bone. In essence, what they meant is that I will keep going until I succeed.

I recognise fear for what it was and I may have had a pity party or two. There were moments when I was mentally exhausted due to the financial stress and the challenge of running a business but on the whole, I embraced every single challenge in 2023 and faced it head-on.

Raising The Bar

My mindset is based on building a legacy and raising the bar. My grandma was my role model and despite all the setbacks and barriers that she encountered, she remained strong. I aspire to be like her. I also want to provide a future for my nieces that they can aspire to and be a role model for future generations. My determining mindset right now where the business is concerned is to be in a position where the not-for-profit aspect of the business that I've set up to build a legacy for my grandma will help break generational barriers to education for children in Ghana. This means a lot to me because my grandma was denied education. I believe that education is a fundamental human right and a way out of poverty. Thus, I want to support others so that they can have an education and they can change their family fortune.

Determinations And Mental Strength

Running a start-up business takes a lot of determination and mental strength. I would advise anybody embarking on a business journey to start by building their mental capacity to be resilient because running a start-up business is a mental exercise. You also need to surround yourself with a selective network of other businesspeople who will support and build you up when you feel isolated or have a sense of imposter syndrome. You may need more than one network for there will be those who may build you up spiritually and those who will give you the commercial direction that you need and share their experiences with you. The key is to build the right network by determining the support structures that you need.

Advice

At times, even your closest loved ones, who are your strongest supporters and genuinely care about your well-being, might be the first to question if running the business is the right path. They might suggest exploring alternative options, especially during periods of financial uncertainty and when you're putting in crazy hours to establish the business, relying on them for financial support. Hence, it becomes crucial to stay unwaveringly focused on your motivation and maintain a steadfast determination to succeed. Additionally, cultivating resilience becomes essential in navigating such challenges.

Resilience in my business has been more than my physical or mental strength. It has involved being in the right place, the right network with the right people and sometimes being exposed to things that I don't know how to do, learning from others and hearing about people's challenges and how they have overcome them has enabled me to build my resilience. I'm also a woman of faith and therefore I build my resilience on the hope that it shall be well, and it is well. Quitting is not an option for me.

The best piece of advice I would give is that in business, there are uncertain and uncharted waters and you may not win the contract immediately and that may present a financial challenge. This is where you must create a strategy for survival.

Where there is no capital and you're unable to raise funds from the banks. You must be creative and innovative with generating an income from other sources and have a strong conviction to keep driving your agenda. However, you must never wait to reach this destination.

It is important to keep reviewing everything you have done. Mistakes will be made but don't give yourself a hard time when it occurs. Take time to ensure that you learn from the mistakes.

Don't be afraid to partner and collaborate with people but make sure they are trustworthy and their values are aligned to yours. Be prepared to take on a part-time job, it may provide some form of capital injection which will allow you the mental space to run your business.

Financial stress can be crippling and it can suck the energy physically and from you rendering you unable to stay motivated and focused. So identifying creative and various ways to raise funds to sustain your business is key. There are a list of jobs from Amazon delivery and Uber Eats to hosting international students that can provide an income stream. Don't pigeonhole yourself into only raising capital from the banks because when that door is shut there's got to be other ways in which you can raise capital and still run your business. Consistently plan to revisit your why, it may transform and evolve as your business transitions.

You will learn and relearn things. One clear message I will offer to female entrepreneurs is a timeless wisdom borrowed from my mother: "No condition is permanent." It means after the rain comes the sun. If you are weathering stormy weather, it will pass. Always remember that nothing stays the same forever.

About Me

Founder and Director of JOA HR Consulting Limited, Jennifer provides customised people management solutions to businesses within health, hospitality, construction, housing and social care. She helps ensure that processes are legally compliant, people-centred and user friendly. Core service offerings include employee relations, employee engagement, policy review and development, and organisational change and training.

Growing up in Ghana, Jennifer was raised by her grandmother who sacrificed her income to keep her in school so that she could receive a good education. Having been denied education herself, her grandmother was passionate about the importance of schooling and the life that it could go on to give you. Eventually, Jennifer was sent to join her father in the UK, where he had fled to seek political asylum. And it was here that she found her passion for HR during a work placement at university where she experienced first-hand the strength and power of employees' voices in shaping and influencing policy development.

Following the loss of her grandmother in 2017, Jennifer's focus has been on living a consciously purposeful life by giving back and impacting lives in order to honour her. Through the success of JOA HR Consulting Limited, she strives to enable her charity, Mary Sowah Foundation, to break the generational cycle of poverty that restricts children from accessing education in Accra, Ghana.

Turning The Impossible Into Possible

Debbie Bryan
Award-Winning Leadership Expert, Podcast Host, International Best-Selling Author, Renowned International TEDx Speaker & Speaker Mentor

"There is always a yes, you just need to go out and find it."
– Debbie Bryan

Have you ever been told not to pursue something that you believed was possible? Me too. Let me tell you how sometimes when you are told no, it does not actually mean no, it means you are asking the wrong person and you need to look harder for the yes.

Let me take you back 13 years ago to when my journey of impossible to possible began. In 2011 my life took a sharp turn. I was living what I thought was my dream life, owning a salon in a luxury health club. I love fitness and sports, not much skill but lots of enthusiasm. My life was amazing, I'd been hairdressing since I was 14, my very first job, until an unexpected event changed everything.

It was an ordinary day, a trip to buy a car that turned into a nightmare. My husband and I tag teamed the drive home to collect what you know as a lemon and I as an old banger, a very cheap car. Having traveled around 35 miles already, imagine my shock and horror when all of a sudden the car lost power while driving on the fast lane on the carriageway. It was 31st January at 7pm at night, dark and cold, I managed to drift the car over to the side of the road and called my husband to suggest perhaps a fuel mishap, noticing that my phone was down to one bar. As my husband pulled in behind me, I jumped out of the car to the petrol cap, (although in hindsight I was not sure I knew how to open it) there was a loud bang and a crash, and a car smashed into him, shunting his car forwards.

But then instead of stopping there, I watched the car curl around its three wheels and hurtle towards me! Knowing that I had nowhere to go, one side of me was the dual carriageway and the other where i thought the car was heading, in those heart stopping moments I thought to myself I am going to die, AND this is probably going to hurt, but in that split second, a surge of determination rose within me—my mind said, NO NO NO I am not going, I am not ready, my boys are not ready. Jake, my 19 year old son at the time, thinks he is ready but he isn't, I can't die and with that I took two steps that saved my life.

The car hit me, leaving me standing but it was like I was standing on ice, I thought: okayt hat wasn't as bad as I thought, before being cuffed on the shoulder and sent spinning. Off balance, I fell to all fours on the road, feeling the carnage of the car smashed up beneath my hands and realizing that I was now in the middle of the dual carriageway. With a second chance of being run over, I thought bugger, I need to move, and crawled to the side of the road.

I just remember thinking, Gosh, it must be bruised because I can't stand on it —there's no blood, just a broken nail! I got to the hospital. I remember them putting me in a bed, they cut everything off—pants, trousers and I remember being laid in a bed and my three boys were standing at the bottom of the bed and thinking you need to move my legs up in the air!

I recall telling them I was badly bruised and Jake said "no Mum, it's definitely broken." And I said "no, no, no, it's just bruised." Anyway, after several X-rays, and possibly quite a lot of painkillers, it was definitely broken so they put me in the ward and said they're going to operate the next day.

The following morning I was approached by the surgeons, at this stage my understanding of a broken leg was a cast for six weeks, everyone signed and then on with your life. So imagine my shock when the surgeon very enthusiastically said to me, we've looked at your X-rays, and we think we can operate, but you're not going to be able to use your right leg.

I just thought WHAT !? No, that can't be true. That can't be right. That can't be what's going to happen. And so I said that can't happen, I have a salon, I need to work and a family to look after! And for some reason the surgeon said okay, and I was left sitting thinking well, I don't know what happened. Later that day, the surgeon returned, this time with much excitement—like they do on TV when they're thrilled about performing surgery—and said, "Okay, we've got a much better plan. You will be able to use the leg, but you won't be able to bend your knee." To my shock, I told them, "I'm a hairdresser. I have a hairdressing salon, I'm in a gym, I've got children I need to drive. That can't be right; that just can't be the answer." Again, he went away.

I think it was just pure fear and pure shock, it wasn't me being argumentative, I had no idea that you had options and then eventually they came back a fourth time and said they could fix the leg and I wouldn't necessarily have a complete degree of bend on my knee. But I will be able to stand on it for periods of time and they were going to take some bone out of my hip. Then the surgeon started saying that they're going to dig deep to get the marrow and I said, "Oh, I'm not a boiled egg." So that was the plan.

All of the time I was in the hospital, I genuinely felt like the luckiest person in the world

Lots of the hospital staff were saying to me "poor you," and I replied "I'm lucky!"

I'm the luckiest person in the world. I should be in the morgue, and I'm here.

This real euphoria gave me a positive mindset. After the operation, they showed me my 2-inch by 10-inch scars on my leg and told me I now had two plates, and 22 screws as well as the injury on my hip, so much for a bruise !

Although I felt pretty lucky, all the while really, I worried about how I could be a hairdresser with a broken leg.

During the two weeks in the hospital, I discharged myself early to get home. There were many more kind deeds and some not so kind, such as a male client being assigned as my nurse for bed pans!

Navigating Life After The Accident

During recovery I thought if I do what they say, I will get back to where I was, for a girl who doesn't love rules that's unusual for me! So the fight began, and my weeks turned into months, non-weight bearing from January to July and longer to be back behind the chair. I struggled to fit into my life. It was frustrating and bewildering, so I turned to the business side as the only thing I could do.

Luckily, by working ON and not IN the business, things moved very quickly. We had hit a turnover of £444 in a million pound spa in just eight months but that's another story.

The Bombshell: Following my recovery, the surgeons wanted to assess my long term recovery and the impact on my future. I felt proud of my progress despite still experiencing pain.

Imagine how I felt when the three top consultants in the country assessed me and told me I would be in a wheelchair by 55!

Shocked and devastated, I realised that the fight was not over. I was going to have to keep fighting. I had the same conviction that I had then that this was not going to be my future. I was not going to be in a wheelchair at 55, and I was going to do everything that I could to fight. I recognised that the healthcare system was set up in a way that is really disempowering and negative for patients. So I had to really try and keep myself positive, and believe in the bigger picture that I could do something that was said to be impossible. That 'no' didn't mean no, it meant to me finding a different way.

Over the following years, I underwent three operations, as well as physiotherapy, while still managing the business. During this time, I would work until my legs swelled so badly I had to crawl up the stairs. I realised that I needed to change my life. I started to look for other ways to work and new markets. By the end I went from a small business owner to the owner of a million pound spa and photography studio, go figure!

Pedalling to Resilience

Business Debbie was thriving and surviving but something was missing, I had long mourned and missed my gym life and felt it was an impossible task to get that back. I tried to join fitness classes but really struggled with getting up off the floor. Some of the moves made me feel like I was an idiot. I stood out like a sore thumb. My body didn't work how I wanted it to, and I didn't have the resilience or physical capability. Until one Saturday, my best friend Jules, sent me an email with the words "Do you fancy this? Rajasthan Golden Triangle in India, total of 360 kilometres, a 10-day trip!" Something in me just thought okay, let's do it!

Now, I'm not a professional cyclist, my friend had to explain the gears! My little legs were spinning and getting nowhere! I didn't understand the kit I ordered a padded women's cycling shorts for comfort and I accidentally purchased a pair of shorts that were a little bit see through. They were super comfy and I even did hundreds of miles around the Cotswolds before discovering that they were actually underwear! Thinking the beeps of the horn were supportive when in reality people could actually see the tattoo on my bum. So I'm definitely not a professional cyclist but I was determined to do this challenge, what I don't have in skill, I make up for in enthusiasm.

When I signed up for the bike ride we had two years to go, plenty of time… then 18 months... then 10 months to go to start training. Reality struck me and the schedule looked grueling, ending up with 50-mile bike rides... *gulp*.

Inspiration time! I listened to a speaker at an event that really resonated and helped my training, a boxer called Amy. She had been asked, "What motivates you to get out and do the hill runs in the morning when it's cold, wet, and the wind's howling?" She said, "Nothing inspires that," But in her head, she knows that if she didn't get up and do the training, then when she gets in the ring, three things are gonna happen: firstly, she's going to get punched; secondly, she will be embarrassed, and thirdly, that she's going to lose, and that will be her own fault because she didn't put the work in.

That really resonated and really stuck with me because this was down to me! It was one hundred percent down to me. The choice of whether I achieved this in India was up to me. Not a physiotherapist or doctor. It's not down to anybody else BUT ME, it's all in my hands.

Receiving the schedules, our first ride was 74 kilometres, the next was 94 kilometres. Additionally, it was a 10-day trip, but only 5 days involved cycling. It then became apparent that these 5 days would consist of very, very hard cycling in India, on roads that are indescribable. It's going to be a bigger challenge.

I needed to take the training seriously. My friend had been on a previous trip where there was a lady in her 70s who had actually completed the ride brilliantly. They have a bus, and when they give you the option of getting on the bus, they will ask if Margaret was on the bus. If she wasn't on the bus, they didn't get on the bus, which Jules regularly reminded me. If you get on that bus, I'm going to call you, Margaret. There was a little good-natured pressure to achieve it, and there was a pressure on myself to achieve this. Summer was cancelled! When it came to barbecues, festivals, and late nights, the sacrifice was done, and I took the training very seriously for the first time in my life. Because I do believe that if you really, really want to do something, and you put the work in, then you can achieve your dreams.

Being the amateur that I was, I trained all summer for India. I was pretty terrified and not very confident I was going to be able to do it. But I made a schedule and really saw an improvement in my fitness. But of course, I had never cycled 5 days in a row, would I come back broken and need that wheelchair after all?

In November, we boarded the plane to India, and with trepidation and nerves kicking in, we arrived at our first hotel. It was fantastic, marking the commencement of our adventure. On the first day, we ventured to Fort Agra in a Tuk Tuk—an experience in itself, with madness, cows, traffic horns—everything you could imagine, but in a busy tourist area. I loved it. The next morning, we rose early to witness the sunrise over the Taj Mahal, capturing a photo on the 'Princess Diana' seat. After this, during lunch and the journey to acquire our brand new bikes, nerves kicked right back in.

Unfortunately, the tour was off to a tricky start. Being really nervous, I went around the corner from everybody else to hide my wobbly start. However, since the bikes were brand new and had to be adjusted, when I turned the handlebars, I almost crashed.

Then our first practice ride, a quick couple of miles on the main road, total culture shock, it was just madness, chaos as road rules are considered suggestions in India.

Of course as I was cycling, my handlebars turned 360 degrees upside down as I was passing six people on a moped with their washing in a sack on top and I had no way to brake or stop on this chaotic road. I carried on biking, perhaps it will fix itself! Finding a path to turn down, our guide fixed the bike as I watched a lady with water on her head greeting us with a smile, turning around to come back, the guide car just parked in the middle of the road, blocking the traffic (remember I said there were no actual rules). Shouting to cross the lanes, we got down to a roundabout and traffic was coming at me from every destination. I started to freeze because I'm still quite phobic on the roads with multiple incoming traffic that doesn't want to stop, the guide yelling at me "JUST PEDAL," afterwards he told me, if you give them a gap, they'll fill it. So I really quickly had to get fairly comfortable on the roads. I remember at breakfast, just being terrified to start the adventure. I thought to myself, oh my god, what have I done? Why, why am I even doing this?

We set off at a pace, with me at the back, everyone was very understanding and the day was broken into four rides, the first 17 kilometres . I remember getting into the first break and starting to think surely we must be close.

It was amazing; all the people from the local village came out and waved at us. Then, in a particular instant, a farm truck adorned with garlands and flowers approached. It was absolutely stunning. The driver stopped just to say hello, and folk music blared out. We even had a little dance before embarking on our next ride. This journey took us through towns and villages, eventually leading us to a village restaurant for lunch. However, to get there, we had to navigate through the village centre, passing by cows, pigs, and camels. It was the only opportunity you would ever get to yell, 'passing camel!' We encountered all sorts of amazing, wonderful, and beautiful scenery along the way.

As we went through these villages, people stood up and applauded us, the kids waved and laughed at us with joy at seeing crazy ladies cycling, I believe it was the first trip since before Covid.

We had some good days cycling and some not so good days, cycling through mountains, sand and terrain so rough it peeled my hard boiled egg for lunch! There was a day where I was chased by some boys. I remember I said to you, I'm not great on the outfit, in the heat and the sweat they react differently it seems, I thought that I had some great outfits to go with me but that was not the case. One day, as I cycled through the muddy village, there was never rain but always mud… we passed a school where the boys had just come out, somehow my shorts decided to roll down, and I couldn't roll them back up, exposing a very white tummy they all just started laughing and chased me, taking pictures and videos! I just peddled as fast as I could get through the village before getting onto the bus and changing my clothes into my spare stuff, high waisted leggings, and even that was pretty tricky when you're in a very hot temperatures and you're on a bus that's got no air conditioning on and you're trying to change lycra. That's a comedy sketch on its own. The memories that we made were massive. I was cycling up a hill huffing and puffing a bit, then there's a lady coming towards me and she's got five sewage pipes on her head. She's barefoot and she's not even breaking the stride while I'm feeling a bit sorry for myself. Now, that's a life lesson in itself, isn't it?

The cycling expedition through India was nothing short of an adventure to treasure forever. Terrifying encounters with traffic, embarrassing wardrobe malfunctions, and the physical strain of challenging terrains tested my resolve. Yet, each obstacle was a stepping stone, each village's applause a reminder of the resilience within.

As I celebrated the finish line on the challenging roads of India, I reflected on the journey—360 kilometres of triumph over adversity. Defying the predictions, I beat the odds and had turned 55 just a few months before and the looming spectre of a wheelchair-bound fate.

The resilience that carried me from a salon owner with a broken leg to a triumphant cyclist defined not just a chapter, but a transformational journey impossible to "I am possible."

I hope you take away that there is always a yes, you just need to go out and find it.

About Me

As an award winning coach of 25 years and qualified NLP Master practitioner and counsellor, Debbie is the Founder of Debbie Bryan International Mastery Coaching. Through her services such as the Success Blueprint™ and Secret CEO Day™, she helps entrepreneurs who are stuck in a cycle of doubt and fear to achieve growth and fall back in love with their business and life.

Debbie's entrepreneurial passion was born when she was just seven years old, selling 12 TVs from her house one afternoon. Since then, she has gone on to work with thousands of entrepreneurs from startups to eight figure businesses in all industries. But this did not come easy…

Having worked as a salon owner, Debbie's whole life turned upside down when in 2011, a life threatening accident left her unable to walk at 55. Despite her setback, her tenacious spirit soon saw her achieve the unthinkable, transitioning from being confined to a wheelchair to cycling an incredible 360 miles across India.

Today, Debbie uses her wealth of experience to provide clarity, assistance and support to others, helping them to overcome and conquer whatever business challenges they may have.

How I Doubled My Turnover (And Team!) During A Global Pandemic

Emma Sansom
Multiple Award-Winning Business Owner
Marketing & Growth Strategy Expert
Flamingo Marketing Strategies Ltd

"Turn your wounds into wisdom" – Oprah Winfrey

This success followed a rollercoaster of twists and turns. It was a period of my life filled with both laughter and tears, and a constant need to keep picking myself up and pushing forward to achieve results. It wasn't easy, but it was definitely worth it. So, I'm going to share with you six valuable lessons I learned during the first two years of running my business. Lessons that I wish I'd known before I started Flamingo, that will hopefully help new or aspiring business owners prepare for the journey and achieve greatness, whether we have another Global Pandemic or not!

It was 7th March 2020. I was basking in the Vietnamese sunshine with my family around me, looking up at the bright blue sky – feeling a huge sense of relief to be taking my first holiday since starting my business.

At this moment in time, I was heading towards the last three months of my first full financial year at Flamingo Marketing Strategies Ltd.

The business had really started to take off within the first nine months. I had signed up several clients for a 'done-for-you' marketing strategy, I'd got all my systems set up and working, and I was making great progress as I threw myself into the depths of the Entrepreneurial world. Fortunately, because my whole career had been in marketing, I never had any concerns on how I'd get the clients and I was also prepared to do whatever it takes to get it off the ground – even if that meant a part-time job to keep the funds coming in. Luckily it wasn't necessary, but what I soon came to realise is you need to be 'better than just your skill' if you want to run a successful business.

As lovely as it would have been to just worry about marketing my business, I had to become an expert in invoicing, business administration, data management, customer service, processes – and more recently as we've grown: HR, insurance, cyber security, leadership and culture – all areas I'd dabbled in through previous roles, but never actually trained in!

So, I had a lot to learn.

Running A Business Is NOT A Piece Of Cake

In fact, statistics show 20% of businesses fail in the first year and 60% within the first three years.

And that's the hard truth about starting a business. It's not easy and it's not for everyone. People who start a business because they want 'freedom' and to choose when they work are in for a real shock, especially in year one. And if the passion – or the commitment – isn't there, there's a risk of becoming part of this statistic.

From another updated resource, the 3 main reasons they fail are:

- **38%** – ran out of cash or failed to raise new capital
- **35%** – there was no market need
- **20%** – were outcompeted

Funny how all three of these reasons link to a reliance on marketing… and yet so many businesses don't do *any* marketing! Which that leads me into my first lesson:

Lesson #1 – Surround Yourself With The Right Support Network

If you know that you can offer a service or product and you have all the skills for the job, but when it comes to finance, strategy, sales and marketing, you have very little or no knowledge – then the first lesson is for you. You don't have to be an expert, but knowing people with different skillsets who are willing to help, advise and support you is invaluable. Failing this, do not be afraid to outsource or bring in someone else into the business who can support you with these areas.

Fortunately, when I started Flamingo, the only area of understanding that I was lacking was the accountancy side but having two amazing parents who ran their own accountancy practice meant that I was covered. When it comes to the numbers and general business advice, who better to have in your corner? Still to this day (5th January 2024 as I write this), they guide and advise me.

As for the business growth side – I listened to podcasts, I went to networking, I spoke to coaches about business growth. I knew that I was never going to be able to figure it all out myself. So, I made sure to invest money in having the right people in place to teach me or at the very least, invest time in learning how other successful entrepreneurs have grown their businesses and commit to being the best I could be at running my business.

I was becoming more and more confident that I was building something to be proud of.

A Very Unexpected Turn Of Events

So, back to the trip to Vietnam. I was around 9 months into running my business and I had decided to take a couple of weeks off and head over to Ho Chi Minh City to see my sister who was living there at the time. During the weeks leading up to the trip we were all feeling nervous because the news channels and our social feeds were being flooded every day about the new COVID-19 outbreaks worldwide, so we worried that we wouldn't make it out to see her before the world went into lockdown, let alone get back again! But we chanced it and got on the flight.

I'd felt proud of my accomplishments during the 9 months of running my marketing company, and I'd even hired a part time member of staff to support me – so it was the perfect opportunity to escape for 14 nights and enjoy some time with my loved ones, getting to experience my sister's new life in Asia.

Little did I know that when I *finally* got back to the UK (because that's another story in itself), the COVID-19 pandemic was going to change everything.

Despite leaving the UK filled with excitement about the year ahead and on track for £100,000 during my first year in business, I came home to absolute chaos – and I'm not talking about the toilet roll shortage (fortunately my neighbour had kindly left some on the doorstep!).

Everything Came Crashing Down

April 2020 – within weeks of the pandemic causing turmoil for UK businesses (including many of my clients) I started receiving the dreaded emails and phone calls:

"Emma, I'm so sorry but we can't operate as normal at the moment. We need to park our services for a few months and see what happens."

"Emma, we've had to close our doors. Our industry has been hit hard. We will have to terminate our contract early, I'm so sorry."

The list went on…

During the following two months, nearly half of the clients had to pause or park our services completely. It was devastating and, in all honesty, I wasn't fully prepared for it. I didn't have a back-up plan if I lost all our clients, apart from the fact I was sensible with money and could cover myself for a few months. When it came to what to do next with the business, I was very much having to 'wing-it' – no Flamingo pun intended.

At the time, it was just me in the business with a part-time employee, who eventually left due to the implications the pandemic was having for her and her need to be at home with her family. Remote working wasn't going to work for us, so I was back flying solo.

Regarding the clients who stayed, the word 'pivot' was used more times in four weeks than I'd heard in my 30+ years of existence, even as a *Friends* addict! But that's exactly what we had to do. We had just launched campaigns targeting schools for one client, airlines for another and the hospitality industry for a third company – three of the most impacted industries from lockdown!

I had to completely think on my feet, park all our hard work and find another way to market these incredible businesses who were feeling huge amounts of pain at this time. I couldn't quite believe what was happening after it being just a few weeks since I was lying on that sunbed feeling like I'd got it all figured out. How wrong I was!

Lesson #2 – Be Prepared To Accept That Things Won't Always Be Easy!

In June 2020, I had to make a choice. Fight or flight.

And I'd worked too damn hard up to this point to cut and run, so I fought! I promised myself when I started Flamingo Marketing Strategies Ltd. I'd do whatever it took to make it a success. And I kept my promise.

Enduring 12 to 16-hour days, minimal sleep and no possible way of getting a work-life balance back, I had to work out what to do next.

Within a couple of months, I'd started to build the business back up and despite feeling nothing at all like a 'fabulous flamingo' and more like a mentally exhausted pigeon, everything started to look a bit better. I even hit my £100k target despite all the uncertainty in the remaining quarter – but then the next issue arose…

I had too much work, to do it all by myself.

And the pandemic was making It very hard to hire!

So, I had to think outside the box.

My other half wasn't happy in her existing role and she wanted to get into marketing. She was incredibly creative and we were living (and therefore bubbled) together. Lightbulb – hire my partner! Makes sense right?

I had a few sleepless nights making long lists of all the pros and cons about whether it could work (because I was scared about it affecting our relationship!). After speaking to my parents to get their advice and confiding in friends about my thoughts, it became quite obvious that given the situation the pandemic has put us in, I should go for it. I didn't really have any other options. If I carried on trying to do it all myself, I was going to lose even more clients or cap my success and not be able to grow.

So I took the chance – and it massively paid off.

Over the next six months, the business really started to take-off again. We were halfway through our second year and the turnover was growing month-on-month.

Having another person with me full-time made a massive difference as we started to replace the clients we had lost. Her work on the website was incredible, we had time to transform our branding, our social media following started to grow and we started doing our own video marketing. Having this support with Flamingo's marketing meant I could really focus on the business development and sales side, whilst still looking after our clients at the same time. One particular project I am still very proud of today which gets circulated every year on 3rd June is a video of me singing a song for my late Nan to celebrate the business's first anniversary on what would have been her birthday.

Working with my other half worked really well… until it didn't.

In December 2020, we broke up. I am by no means saying the business caused this because there were other reasons why we eventually decided to split up, but when you're working AND living with your partner and not really seeing anyone else due to the lockdown rules, it's a bit intense. Pair this with long hours and challenging days at work – it was bound to have a bit of a knock-on effect.

Lesson #3 – Avoid Working With Partners, Family, or Friends

So, we had to call it a day, which naturally caused a bit of a bump in the road (just as things were getting better for the business!) and also links to lesson 2 – *be prepared to accept things won't always be easy!*

After a three-and-a-half-year relationship, it was heart-breaking to have to go our separate ways. I wanted to support her financially whilst she found a new job so I ensured she had the time to do that. She moved out and we both had to get used to living alone, and for me, I was flying as a solo Flamingo again – and the business was booming… so I had to do something about it because it wasn't possible to do everything alone.

But before I move on to that, I don't want to ignore how important lesson three is. I know it works in some cases; my parents are a fine example of that. However, after the experience I went through where it's impossible to keep business and personal separate – especially when there's a break-up involved – here's my advice: if a friend or family member wants to start a business with you or join yours, don't do it!

Business is business, and personal is personal – but when you put them together, *everything* becomes personal and the next thing you know, you might be treading on eggshells not saying what you really think, be afraid to deal with poor performance, or you might even realise they aren't as good as you think. It might seem like a good idea at the time – but what happens if you have to fire them?

Fortunately, with my scenario, it was purely the breakup that meant she started to look for another role to move on to. She was brilliant at her job and we loved working together, but it was never going to work long-term. You can't work with your ex and not expect issues somewhere along the line! Four years later, we have both moved on and are with new partners, leading very happy lives.

Time To Build My Army!

The business was heading back in the right direction, we'd hit the £100k mark in year one, and in January 2021 we were just six months away from finishing year two. I knew that I needed a wingman or woman to support me, which is when

Chris came along as my 'Marketing Manager' just a few weeks later, who is still with me today and is now my 'Head of Marketing and Clientele'.

Before I explain how Chris and I stormed our way to the £220k mark after he joined in February 2021, I still had one little hurdle to jump over first. A little hiccup of a recruitment decision. We'll call her 'Polly'.

Polly joined in January 2021 and was with me for just two weeks in total before she handed her notice in. After taking the work laptop off the premises the night she resigned, she then went on to set up a competing marketing and events agency, just one week later. *Lovely girl.*

At the time, it was another bit of salt rubbed in the wound. I was very aware that I knew nothing about this person so naturally fear kicked in. I had worked so hard for 18 months to risk it being destroyed. Worst-case – she may have taken copies of all of my work from the laptop before it was returned. She might have been trying to poach my clients – I'll never know! At this point I was more annoyed at the aggravation it was causing than anything else, because I still needed another person to help me and I was back to square one.

The only saving grace was that I knew how hard it was to get a business off the ground, building it up from scratch and that it really isn't for everyone. So, I tried not to let it worry me and focus on my own business and moving it forward. Sure enough, within 18 months her business had dissolved and Flamingo was continuing to thrive.

Lesson #4 – Protect Your Empire!

The reason I'm sharing this is because it's amazing just how much had happened in the first 18 months of running my business, that right now (four and a half years in) has become so insignificant and unimportant as the business has evolved, but at the time was a true test of resilience and every single setback felt like the end of the world. This is the side of launching a business that people don't see – the wild rollercoaster ride that I was never going to get off but my god, the twists and turns were unexpected at times!

The lesson learnt from this was that I made sure anyone who joined my team had gone through a three-step interview process (including tasks submitted to check quality). I also updated the contractual agreement about setting up competing businesses, poaching clients, access to work files etc., to give me a bit more reassurance. So from this recruitment mistake, I learnt how to cover my back in case it happened again. Now, with the policies and contracts, and the incredible HR partner I've got, I'll never be this vulnerable again!

So now it's February 2021. Polly had gone, Chris had joined, and little did I know at this stage that together we were going to be a force to be reckoned with. He was just the sort of person I needed!

Despite it being over a year since the first lockdown, we still weren't out of the woods when it came to the long-standing damage caused by the pandemic. For our new clients, we came up with innovative ways to make their companies stand out (after all, that's our motto!) and worked exceptionally hard to find the people who still needed their services. I was back to working ridiculously long hours, but this time I had an ally. Some days we worked way into the evening, we pushed our marketing hard and found ways to build up our client base again. It actually became the start of a wonderful friendship because it felt like it was us against the world – racing to the finish line of year two and seeing what we could achieve!

The relationships I had with my clients pre-COVID were hard to create with new clients due to the remote ways of working. The coffee dates and the trips to their office stopped, the meetings with their full teams stopped. So, with the newer clients, we naturally felt disconnected in comparison to our existing ones, and that brought its own challenges. But we worked through it, and we did everything we could to keep them happy and provide value to their businesses.

Lesson #5 – You Get Out What You Put In

We worked harder than we would have needed to had the pandemic not hit – but it paid off because things started to feel a little less stressful as we onboarded a few more clients and found ways to save our existing ones. By this point we were just a couple of months away from the end of our second year…

… and just when everything looked like it was picking up and our numbers were looking strong for the end of year two, one of the marketing tools we used completely changed its structure and capabilities, meaning we had to offer a reduced level of service – which, you guessed it – reduced the invoice value we could charge our clients each month. So, it meant their bills were cut in half and I had to find a way to replace that income! I was back on the rollercoaster!

When was I going to catch a break?

At the time, I was still working from home. I specifically remember lying on the spare bed in the back bedroom where my desk was set up, having a little cry (we all do it!) whilst my amazing Mum came and laid beside me, helping me figure out what to do next and how to navigate the changes.

Her exact words were, "Emma, you've survived worse – you'll get through this, you always do," and she was right. I'd been on one hell of a journey since I launched Flamingo in June 2019 and I was still here. It hadn't folded, despite the pandemic, while many other businesses had.

This is where everything started to change – and my sixth and final lesson was learnt.

Lesson #6 - Get Up, Shake It Off, And Move On

This lesson I can thank my family for really, because it's with their love and support – massively backed by the fact they are retired accountants and knew my numbers – that I had the confidence to carry on fighting!

Crying helped of course, but moping for days wasn't going to. I had to remember that I was still in a fortunate position where my business could still survive.

So, we made the changes we needed to do, adapted our packages to suit, then carried on hunting for new business to bring the numbers back up.

Within the next two months we finished the year stronger than we could have ever imagined – which was such a massive accomplishment when I think back to the year before when I'd just lost half my clients within a few weeks.

All of our hard work had started to pay off.

We recruited a third Flamingo, we invested in an office and our earnings for the first month of year three were even better than our BEST month of the previous year.

Once we had moved into our office, a beautifully-renovated barn in Warwickshire, we started to attract much bigger companies. It meant that we could invite them over once the rules changed and face-to-face meetings were allowed again. It meant that we were taken more seriously as a business, rather than 'just' a back bedroom start-up.

Three staff soon became four.

Fast-forward to January 2024, we are now a team of six (recruiting for a seventh!), we are on track for £500k this financial year and we've probably learnt a hundred more lessons along the way than the six I've shared here from the first two years.

The main one of course being – resilience really is key when it comes to running a business. Just keep looking ahead and to quote Oprah Winfrey – "Turn your wounds into wisdom".

That's what I've done, and I hope my story will help you find the strength if you're on your own rollercoaster ride right now to be resilient and keep fighting to reach the light at the end of the tunnel.

About Me

After launching my marketing business 'Flamingo Marketing Strategies Ltd' back in June 2019, my journey to success has had many twists and turns, and we're only four and a half years in!

Prior to Flamingo, I graduated with a Marketing degree from Leeds University, and I've worked in marketing for over 12 years. Starting at 21 years old as a Marketing Assistant at an Engineering company in Coventry, and building my way up to more senior roles such as Head of Marketing for a large marketing agency as well as a global software company, I had to work with a lot of different industries and my love for marketing continued to grow.

Based in Leamington Spa, Warwickshire, I run a multi award-winning agency that offers 'done-for-you' marketing services to allow you to stand out from your competition, much like a Flamingo stands out in a flock of pigeons. My aim is to continue to build a business that helps Business Owners reach their full potential, by supporting them with their marketing strategies. I have an incredible team and we're able to cover all areas of marketing, as well as consultancy and training. I also deliver talks on all areas of marketing and business growth.

I decided to share my story in the Queens In Business series because if even just one of the lessons from my first two years in business helps you make smart choices when it comes to running your business, then it was worth writing about.

My chapter is dedicated to my incredible family who have supported me every step of the way, and to you, the reader, whose journey may only just be beginning – I hope it becomes the best story you ever tell.

Defying Odds And Walking To The Beat Of My Own Drum

Vanessa Frater-Robertson
Multi-Award-Winning International Speaker,
Confidence Coach & Communication Consultant
Vanessa Frater Robertson Coaching -
The Confidence Core

"You don't get what you want - you get what you believe!"
– Vanessa Frater-Robertson

I'm a qualified confidence coach and I specialise in coaching women in their forties - and over, for whom past traumas are continuing to hold them back from achieving their career, relationship and life goals.

I feel fulfilled and at one with my purpose because now I'm coaching and training other women in business, Mumpreneurs and Femalepreneurs to find their "why" their purpose, and achieve their big bodacious goals without that female or mum guilt!

So why is this so important to me? How can I help these women? Well, having overcome mental trauma myself and benefitting from strategies to rediscover and grow my own confidence and coaching techniques that have changed my life, I am well placed to empower women to live their best lives.

My desire to help women who are in a similar position to where I was, drives me to continually improve my knowledge and listen more to what they want. I know what it's like to feel alone not knowing which way to turn to change your life. Sometimes it isn't easy to ask for help because we think we should know how to do this for ourselves. The key is to realise that everyone needs help at some point in their lives, and there is no shame seeking help to break through the status quo and transform your life.

Have you ever looked at your life and asked yourself the following questions?:

"How am I still in the same position I was a few years ago?"
"How have I not progressed to where I want to be?"
"Why am I so scared to take action?"

I get it, as I've asked myself those same questions. I feel truly blessed to be able to help women gain the clarity on where they want to go and get unstuck from what's holding them back. Encouraging them to take back the reins of their power by becoming accountable, responsible, and the creator of their own confidence is a way for me to impact their lives in a positive way.

My Story: The Journey To The Real Me

You might be wondering how did I start my entrepreneurial journey? Well let me take you back…

It is December 2006 - it's bitterly cold and Jack Frost is working overtime. Commuters are breaking out their gloves and oversized scarves and some are putting their car engines on to heat up before they drive off to face the day. It's the type of morning that's crisp and cold but the sun is absolutely dazzling and very low in the sky so drivers wear sunglasses to avoid getting blinded by the sun.

I'm sitting in a very modern, fairy swish, open plan new office building. It's got beautiful glass partitions and all the mod cons. I can hear the clink of the coffee mugs as work colleagues are getting their morning drinks and the smell of the high-grade sustainable coffee is welcome as it wafts over to me. This multinational organisation has the best workforce in the industry, but I don't feel like the best. I feel quite beaten down.

My line manager, a small petite, brown curly-haired Australian ball of fun is pleased with my work, and she congratulates me on my latest employee communications campaign.

"Very well done Vanessa!"

"Comments from employees are saying that the campaigns really helped them understand more about the company and the vision. By making it more engaging and fun, it has actually helped them understand where they fit in the grand scheme of things! Very well done!"

But not everyone is delighted with my work. Like the dark cloud he is, his 6ft frame comes into the office and it feels as if the air has been sucked out of my lungs - I inhale sharply as if I'm bracing for impact!

"Vanessa! A word – my office now!"
Oh, morning to you too I think to myself.

He looks a little bit like Clarke Kent before he turns into Superman, but his eyes are cold like flint and when he smiles the warmth doesn't reach them. He sits back in his chair, and it seems like his frame takes up the whole of the space. He's so tall that his legs look too long for the ultra-modern art deco chair he is sat in. I feel uncomfortable as he makes me wait for what seems like an eternity before he motions for me to sit down

"Vanessa. How long you been with us now?"
He doesn't wait for me to respond.

"Oh, about 10 months, isn't it? How do you think it's going? Well, you've done a campaign and that did get a little bit of engagement, but it's NOT all about the campaigns There are other things that need to be done!"

There are many more interactions like this whittling me down and chipping away at my confidence making me feel like my work isn't worthwhile. Near the end it was like death by a thousand paper cuts – not one interaction was enough to take me out, but the effect was a negative build up making it impossible to focus.

There was a time when he believed a piece of my work was done by someone else and he had nothing but praise for that work.

"Ah Tony, this work is fantastic. It absolutely encapsulates what we're trying to do at this company and what we're trying to achieve and the employees are going to love it!"

"Oh actually Dan, Vanessa did that piece of work"

"Did she? Oh well there are some other things that actually really need to be done and it's not quite finished yet…and yes there are some real major holes! Vanessa, can you make sure that the last section is strengthened and on my desk by 9:00 am tomorrow morning? Excellent!"

And it goes on and on and on like this for a further few months. I regret my decision to take this contract and to extend it when things were going well after my successes in the initial campaign. Everything I'm doing is being torn to shreds by the HR Director. I realise he wants me out and he starts a behaviour pattern to manage me out of the organisation. It gets so bad that my line manager suggests, off the record, that I should go for a compromise agreement just to get out from under his gaze and from under his attacks. I realise that this is probably my only way out and with a heavy heart I take the compromise agreement and the payoff which buys my silence, because it's the only way for me to leave with my dignity intact without being destroyed.

Have you ever had a situation that broke your spirit and completely smashed your confidence?

Delay, Denial And Distraction!

The next 14 days following my departure from the company saw me in a daze. I'm sleeping in, not eating properly, and avoiding my friends. My husband is taking our eighteen month old - baby to nursery so that I can rest. I am feeling sorry for myself, beating myself up and blaming myself for everything that went wrong - even the things that were out of my control.

I'm listening to that vicious, vindictive, vitriolic voice in my head that's telling me" STAY IN YOUR lane - don't do anything NEW- because YOU failed!!!"

I believe in this voice with every fibre of my being,but I don't want my story to be I can't do this, I want it to be I can do this! So I start listening to webinars and watching YouTube videos on how to rewire your brain and re-fire your brain: change your story and change your life ...but there's still a part of me that feels a little bit like a loser!

At this dark period in my life, my best friend Sarah calls me and suggests a coffee. Sarah is about 5ft 9ins - and has -long flowing brown hair that she wears- in a bun on the top of her head. She's got a wicked sense of humour, and she knows where my bodies are buried, figuratively speaking of course!

"Vanessa what happened to you? You were the life and soul of the party at school. You were the entertainment rep in sixth form and was the shoulder to cry on when friends had a problem."

"Sarah I'm procrastinating - I feel so stuck and I don't want to be here. I feel like I'm in my own personal prison cell and I can't find the key!"

"Vanessa, I always thought that you could be a coach working for yourself because you're always willing to help people. I was listening to Psychology Today on Radio Four or something and it says that procrastination isn't really the reason that's stopping you. It is probably the fear underneath: fear of failure or maybe fear of success if you try something new. So, Vanessa, what are you scared of?"

Has anybody ever said something that seems like the clouds part and the sun shines a light onto the real situation?

Resilience Is A Choice!

Things were not easy for me over the next few months and I knew I had a decision to make! My decision? I want to guide and coach women to become better versions of themselves and truly reach for the ideal life that would inspire them to achieve greatness.

My Mum wants me to settle down into a nine to five job, but she doesn't understand the pain that I was in. She doesn't understand staying put in that pain was more painful than going through the discomfort to go towards my ideal life.

I don't listen to the negativity and little by little things start to change. I go to The Coaching Academy, and I complete the Personal Performance Diploma and a specialist Confidence Coaching course. Online training, assessments, hundreds of hours of coaching training and delivery ensue, and 18 months later I receive my coaching accreditation.

Speaking engagements to support my coaching start coming my way, I'm getting nominations for speaking awards, I'm winning awards and I'm speaking on international stages! Things are turning around and I'm amplifying my voice to encourage women to use theirs. I start to take my clients through my Transformative Life Launchpad programme because I can help them go from a position of overwhelm and low confidence towards their ideal life. This is my purpose, my dream and my life and I feel a sense of fulfilment when my clients get the breakthroughs they need, to take the courageous steps towards their life's dreams.

My Legacy

Empowering women in business, Mumpreneurs and Femalepreneurs to step into their confidence is my passion.

I realise you don't get what you want in life: you get what you believe. Life is like the weather, and you never fully anticipate what is around the corner. With the rain you get pain and with the sun you get joy. When those two things come together, you get rainbows which can lead you to your ideal life.

My transformation to a more confident Mumpreneur version of me was not an overnight occurrence. It took months of healing, self-development and learning from successful people to help me get to the next level on my journey.

One of the major things standing in my way was me! I wasn't aware that I was confusing the source of self-esteem and self-confidence. I thought that my past determined my future and that my past failures meant that I was a failure or a bad person. How wrong I was. I knew that I needed help to gain clarity on the direction I wanted to go in life. What I didn't know was that to unlock the potential within me, I had to unravel the negative stories I was telling myself. They were sucking the energy I needed for the new positive and confident life journey I desired.

By engaging with a few coaches, they raised my awareness of what was holding me back and I was able to take the first steps to change my life and start to influence the outcomes I wanted. I learnt that confidence in things that I did was not the same as what I believed about myself and how I valued myself i.e. self-esteem.

The realisation was like a dazzling light bulb going on and shining a light on the shadows in my mind. I found that my imposter syndrome type, which was perfectionism, got in the way of fulfilling my full potential because I could never believe anything I did was good enough or that I was valid unless something was perfect. This was definitely about my self-esteem and I found that I could change the way I viewed myself through positive mantras, transformative coaching and spending time in the company of people who wanted to change their lives for the better just like me. Being honest with myself was also vitally important. Facing up to the truth was sometimes very uncomfortable or even painful but I was glad I did it as I got the best results from the learning process.

I became more interested in the concept of self-confidence and how it was built around my skills and capabilities to do something. So if something in my life failed and my confidence faltered, I started to see that it wasn't me that was the failure but that this was a necessary learning opportunity and a chance to grow and improve my skills. My self-esteem was fully intact and didn't take a hit because I didn't equate failures with a lack of self-worth anymore. What I believed about myself was the basis for my self-esteem and I got into the habit of depending on my own internal validation for a job well done, acceptance of myself and self-love. Although external validation was welcome, reliance on it to feel worthy is precarious as its source is unreliable and in some instances finite. I also abandoned the futile path toward perfection and set my sights on the achievable path to excellence. These learnings were truly the turning point on my confidence journey and I'm very grateful that I gathered the courage to take the necessary first steps.

The Path To Success

One of my coaches says: "success leaves clues" and to me that means observing the evidence trail of people I want to engage with or learn from. This is an effective way to become familiar with what it takes to become successful. I have found that confidence is a big part of this success evidence, which comes with time i.e., building up your skillset and consistent action to get the things done that need to be done. Understanding the science behind success and what it means for me and my own journey has truly been a game changer.

My transformation coaches have all coached me on the personal and character traits that constitute an extraordinary person. I'm extremely grateful to them for opening my eyes to becoming a lifelong student of personal transformative change, to keep showing up as the best version of me so that I can help those who seek my help. What I'm learning on this journey is so important and I'm having fun doing it. I came across a quote from Miguel de Cervantes' Don Quixote, which illustrates this point beautifully:

"The joy is on the road not the inn."

What drives me to succeed?

You may be thinking what drives me and keeps me reaching for what I want.

I developed my life vision and visualised what I wanted in all areas of my life. This helped me clarify what was most important to me and I discovered it's easier to say no to things that don't align with my life vision and have more time for the things that do.

It's easy to keep motivated when things are running smoothly and the weather is nice and bright outside. When days are dark, depressing and uninspiring or everything seems so hard to accomplish, motivation alone does not work. I needed to dig deep and know what was driving my deepest purpose and why. Joe Stump and Dean Graziosi use an exercise called seven --levels deep, to help you get crystal clear clarity on what your biggest "why" is. Someone asks you what the most important goal to you is and then they ask you a total of seven - times why you want it. For the first few levels you are in your head with very logical answers. If you get someone to do this with you, I'll bet by the time you get to level five or six -of answering the questions, you'll be in your heart and you'll become more emotional.

When I did this, my first level cliché answer was financial freedom but as I kept asking myself why I wanted financial freedom, I finally got to the seventh- level and it was: providing freedom (choices) for my family and setting out a blueprint for success for my children. This is my deepest "why" and I was in floods of tears once the reasons became more specific and heartfelt. Once the emotion of my deepest "why" was attached to my vision and goals, it helped me stay focused and committed to my life vision and soul-calling passion. It is stronger than motivation and willpower and I can achieve things even when I don't feel like doing something. It's the kind of emotion and anchoring that will see you keep going when a stronger person without a strong "why" will give up.

It is also the emotional anchoring that has helped me get through the lack of belief from some peers or people in authority over me. I was always taught to be polite and not ruffle too many feathers (I didn't always listen to this). But I was also taught to grab every educational opportunity and be strong because that was what would set me free from passive aggressive gaslighting, which could have held me down. If I had entertained the naysayers in my life I wouldn't have written this chapter, I wouldn't have helped the women who needed me and I wouldn't be thinking about my next steps to help even more women have the impact in their lives that they desire. It hasn't been an easy journey but I thank God and my family for believing in me and giving me the strength to shine as bright as I want, work with the contracts and people I want and to keep moving no matter what!

It all starts with belief in yourself!

I cannot stress the next point enough: once you know what you want to do, believe in yourself even when others don't. All success starts with a belief that you can do what you want to achieve. If you don't believe it, it won't happen. Expecting others to always get the vision that was given to you, will sap your energy and allow self-doubt to creep in. Some people need to see the evidence of vision before they believe it. So please protect your dreams so that you have the space and time to do what's necessary to make them become a reality, without them being ripped apart by people who don't get what you're doing at the outset. You might not get everything you want straight away, but you'll never get something you don't believe in – here's that saying again:

"you manifest what you believe, not what you want"

Whatever you decide to do, get crystal clear on your deepest "why" because on the days when motivation has evaporated, and when things get tough, you'll need something stronger and meaningful to you to keep you going towards your vision. When you know what your deepest "why" is, keep learning and honing your craft to become the best at what you do. True lasting confidence comes with patience through practising your craft, skill and developing and implementing your knowledge. It will take time to build the capability and the certainty in order to gain this confidence. Aim to do something until you can't get it wrong, not just until you get it right.

The next step on from belief and knowing your deepest "why" is to then get clarity on how you're going to achieve your vision or dream. It is important to do it in this order as you don't want the "how" to scupper the vision/dreaming phase but you also need a dose of reality to break the big dream down into manageable chunks that are stretching you, but not so overwhelmingly big that they have you running for the hills. I want you to succeed and not give up because the task was too scary because it wasn't broken down to the micros steps needed. This step is vital as a dream will remain a dream without the action needed to make them come to fruition.

Get Into ACTION!

You'll also face challenges that seem so overwhelming, when doing something new, that you might become scared to continue. This is when you'll need to know that courage isn't doing things without fear, it is doing something even when you are scared and learning more and more about what's required on your journey. Getting into action will help you overcome the fear even if it doesn't completely get rid of it. Many coaches say: "action is the antidote to fear" and I also believe that is true. Some days you'll achieve major leaps and then others only one step towards what you want or none at all – the key is to not give up and keep going. Martin Luther King said it best:

> "If you can't fly then run, if you can't run then walk,
> If you can't walk then crawl but whatever you do
> you have to keep moving forward!"

If it's the right path for you, you can do this. Most importantly, because you're reading this, I believe that you have everything inside you to be successful. We are here on this Earth and we all have a purpose. It may take some people longer to find it or go through different seasons where they achieve different things, but with time and patience your true

North will become clear. If it is something that makes your heart sing, even better, because when you enjoy what you do, the people you serve will feel this energy and benefit from it. I also believe that true abundance (in all categories of our lives) comes from doing the things we enjoy. Deepak Chopra encapsulates this belief in a beautiful quote:

"Chase the goddess of joy and the goddess of abundance will get jealous and follow".

I dedicate this chapter to my two boys, Kai and Connor. Remember my boys, always believe in yourselves, and walk to the beat of your own drum!

About Me

Vanessa is a qualified confidence coach and multi-award-winning international speaker. She specialises in coaching Women in Business, Mumpreneurs and Femalepreneurs, in their forties and over, for whom difficult obstacles are continuing to hold them back from achieving their career, relationship and life goals. She empowers them to develop success action plans for sustainable businesses guilt free!

To find out more about how Vanessa helps you overcome the obstacles holding you back from a truly confident life, visit her website for more information. You can book an initial enquiry call or an in-depth discovery session for a more comprehensive session.

https://vanessafraterrobertson.com/

Rising Stronger

Charlotte Cheetham
Gut Health Coach
Lifeinsights

"You may not control all the events that happen to you, but you can decide not to be reduced by them." – Maya Angelou

I am a gut health coach. I help stressed business women going through the menopause how to manage their digestive distress, so that they learn how to change their lifestyle to allow them to gain more energy, lose weight, sleep better, concentrate better and enjoy their relationships with food, friends and family again.

The Trials And Tribulations Of Being Married To The Forces

It took me over 30 years to understand that I was not stupid, lazy or useless.

As the sixth of eight children, I spent almost every day being told by my parents and teachers that I would never be clever enough to go to University. I was always told that I could do better, that I could try harder, that I needed to pay more attention in class and that I wasn't good enough to succeed in life.

I went to Oxford to train as a registered nurse. When I qualified my senior tutor said to me "Well, there's a turn up for the books. We all thought you would fail your exams. After all, you're not very clever are you?" Immediately after qualifying I got married to a RAF officer who was a pilot.

For the first five months we lived in married quarters near Rutland Water. I didn't drive. I was in the middle of nowhere and didn't know anyone. I was expected to attend coffee mornings on the RAF base and to support my husband's career at all costs. During that time I fell pregnant with my first child. Over the next nine months we moved from Rutland to Doncaster and then to Cornwall where my first child was born.

When my son was 3 months old we moved to north Scotland. It was cold, snowy and very grey. We moved into a house on the RAF base with old metal framed windows and storage heaters that used up all the heat by ten in the morning. The walls were painted beige, the carpets were beige and the curtains were all brown.

It was a long, cold winter and my husband spent long hours away flying. It was a very lonely existence being in North Scotland. I was nowhere near any family or friends. My son cried all the time and never slept. Slowly, I became depressed and struggled to cope with getting up in the morning. I didn't feel as if I had any purpose in life. I didn't know anyone and I felt as if my life was falling to pieces. My son only slept for a few hours each day. I didn't want to go out and I hardly saw my husband. Each day was a struggle through which I could see no end.

However, a year after moving up to Scotland we bought our first house and moved out of RAF quarters into a warm, well insulated house.

At last I could keep warm during the day. I had neighbours who would babysit so I could go out with my husband and I started to get to know people in the cul de sac in which we lived. However, my son continued his poor sleep pattern so I spent every day feeling exhausted. As a consequence of this my depression returned. I also suffered from gut problems. I no longer wanted to leave the house as I was worried that I would need access to toilet facilities or that I would suffer from abdominal cramps and not enjoy being out.

Life became more isolating and difficult to manage until I visited my GP. He prescribed antidepressants which started to kick in after a couple of weeks. My thoughts became more lucid and I was able to concentrate better. As a result of the improvement in my mental health, I managed to find a job working in outpatients in Inverness. At the time that was my life saver! I had a great childminder and I was doing something that I enjoyed doing while knowing that my son was being looked after by someone who he loved to stay with. I had learnt that working in a job I enjoyed, had given me the confidence to let me be who I am without beating myself up, thinking I was not good enough to be a parent. I also wished I had had the courage to speak to my GP earlier so that I could have had more relief from antidepressants earlier on.

As my husband's career constantly changed, we kept moving house every six to twelve months which was challenging. However, it was to become even more challenging in 1990 when my husband was sent for a scan in Wiltshire following a deterioration in his hearing. He had previously enjoyed flying as a pilot on Nimrods in Scotland and was now a flying instructor teaching university students to fly on a University Air Squadron.

Following his scan he was informed that he had an acoustic neuroma which is a benign tumour. He was immediately grounded from flying and had to undergo surgery to have the tumour removed. He was admitted to the London Hospital in Whitechapel. He had one of the best Neurosurgeons in the world operating on him, but he had a 50/50 chance of having a facial droop afterwards and slurred speech so it was a very scary time not knowing what the outcome of the surgery would be.

It took 16 hours for the surgery to be performed and two weeks in hospital to recover from the operation. Through surgery he had lost the hearing in his left ear and was potentially prone to balance problems. During his stay in hospital I visited him every day but that meant the sacrifice of leaving my four year old son at home being cared for by grandparents while having my daughter with me who was still only a baby.

After returning home it took him three months to recover sufficiently before he could return to work. He was grounded from flying for an indefinite period, not knowing whether he would ever be able to fly again. He was posted to RAF Valley in Anglesey where he worked as a ground instructor for the flying school there, where flying students were learning to fly fast jets. Following a period of nine months of teaching, he attended a medical assessment where he was given his flying category back meaning he could fly as or with a copilot. He was consequently posted to Oxfordshire where he began a tour flying VC10 tankers. Such a relief for him to regain his flying category, and a relief for me to know that he could continue his flying career for another few years without having to be medically retired.

Watching my husband's recovery taught me that patience is definitely a virtue even if it meant moving house to the middle of nowhere in Wales! By this time I was 30 years old. In order to prove to my parents, teachers and family that I was not stupid, I decided to study with the Open University. This was the beginning of a fundamental change in my view of myself and life.

Studying And Managing Emotions With Sick Children

I began to realise that I did have the ability to study at degree level, although at the time I hadn't actually thought about getting a degree. I studied health subjects as I was unable to work as a nurse all the time, so the studying was really to keep up to date with current health practices so that I could keep my nursing registration. I started to mix with other students during weekend lectures which gave me food for thought and gave me the impetus to gain more qualifications. Little did I know that this would set me up to be the eternal student for the rest of my life!

One of the most cathartic and enjoyable weeks I have ever had, occurred when I was studying psychology. I had a summer school at Durham University and was able to enjoy the week as a student. I wasn't a mum and I wasn't a nurse. I could immerse myself in study mode without having any other responsibility for anything else! It was bliss!

However, it wasn't long before I was again struggling with life. Sleepless nights were back on the agenda with my third child and my daughter who was five at that time was struggling with her educational development. Although she was happy in herself, it was evident that she was not able to concentrate for long periods. She would suddenly lose concentration and go blank. At the time we didn't know why she was doing that, and we didn't know either that we would be facing more heartache and years of trialling different medications to control her condition.

After another three years and four house moves later, we were living in Hertfordshire. My husband had left the RAF and was living as a civilian at last. I was finally able to enjoy a life away from the military and able to develop my career.

At least, that's what I thought. No such luck! My youngest son started to develop serious upper respiratory infections and was constantly taking courses of antibiotics. Eventually he had surgery to have his tonsils removed and grommets inserted into his ears. He could finally hear properly and start to catch up on his education.

At the same time my daughter started to have seizures. She had a MRI scan after which we were shocked to find out that she was suffering from a tumour which was triggering them. Surgery was not an option at that time because the tumour area was too near the brain stem so was too dangerous to operate.

We embarked on a long journey over seven years taking her to Great Ormond Hospital for visits to see the Neurologist. The medication wasn't working and she reached a point in her life whereby she was having seizures on an almost daily basis. Every time she had a seizure her memory was wiped. She was unable to eat and digest food so had to have special drinks prescribed by the GP. It was so tough to see her suffering so much. She was bullied at school every day because of her seizures. She was put into the bottom group of pupils at school and told she was a nonachiever because of her epilepsy. She was not allowed to go on school trips and was slowly alienated from everyone around her. Her only saviour was going to drama school at weekends where she loved to sing and dance until that too, had to stop because of her seizures.

Being a mum I was expected to be the main carer. My husband had a job as an IT Systems Analyst, worked long hours and was unable to leave his job to help with child care. I managed to find a job in occupational health but was constantly having to leave each day to collect my daughter from school every time she had a seizure.

This situation continued until my daughter was fifteen years old. It was a tough few years. There were no local support groups and as my daughter suffered from a very rare tumour there was nobody with any knowledge about the issues surrounding the condition. Life became a trial and my resilience was continually ebbing while I struggled to manage the health issues being presented by my daughter.

As time went on with trying to cope with bringing up three children, working, studying and looking after a child with a neurological condition life became fraught. I was suffering from intense gut issues due to the anxiety I was experiencing from living through this nightmare situation. I didn't want to go out and socialise due to the fear of being ill myself while I was out. At the same time I was feeling very isolated.

When my daughter reached fifteen years old the Neurosurgeons at Great Ormond Hospital decided that they would try to operate to remove the tumour as her epilepsy had become uncontrollable with drugs. She was admitted to the neuro ward and taken down to theatre. They inserted a small computer block into her brain to measure the activity of the nerves in her brain and then sent her back to the ward.

However, two days later she fell into a coma. She was taken to intensive care where she was placed on a ventilator. It was the scariest moment of my life watching her unconscious with tubes coming from everywhere and not knowing whether she would survive.

Being a nurse gave me more knowledge than I wanted to know. I knew what could go wrong. I was in floods of tears and the sister of the intensive care unit just told me to pull myself together and stop crying. I don't think I have come across such an unsympathetic nurse in my life. I wasn't coping well with the trauma of watching my child suffer but knew that I had to dig deep to be positive in front of her.

After twenty four hours in intensive care my daughter was taken back to theatre where she was found to have had a bleed into her brain due to a blood vessel that had been damaged during the first surgery. It was a real shock as we did not know how it would affect her brain or her life in the long term.

After removing the bleed in her brain the surgeons went on to remove the tumour. She remained unconscious in intensive care for another twenty four hours before the doctors tried to wake her... It was a slow and scary process watching her wake up. We had no idea whether she would be able to understand anything once she did. It took another twenty four hours before she was able to communicate with us. She slowly came round and was able to mumble a few sounds but unable to talk.

It took another day before she was able to communicate coherently. She was moved back to the ward once she woke up but didn't want to eat and showed signs of being very depressed. To watch your child undergo such difficult surgery is heartbreaking. If only I could have been in her place instead!

One week later she was discharged from hospital as it was thought that she would recover better at home. It had been a long two weeks as we were commuting in and out of London from Hertfordshire on a daily basis during that time, as we also had the responsibility of looking after our youngest son.

When she returned home she began the uphill struggle of recuperating from the surgery. Slowly she regained her appetite and started to show more interest in life. She had homeschooling for six months before eventually returning to school. Her seizures started to diminish and she became happier in herself.

Six months after her surgery she returned to school. She sat her GCSE exams and then waited for her results. Being in the bottom set for all subjects her teachers had written her off, expecting her to fail everything. Surprisingly, she got 100% in her Maths GCSE. Although it was not so surprising for us as she had spent seven years studying Maths through Kumon classes where she did a lot of repetitive learning.

Getting Back To A More Normal Life

Life for all of us gained a sense of normality. My daughter went to college and I was once more able to find a job as an occupational health advisor.

Our sons continued in their education and life became more manageable. My health also started to improve as I was no longer going through all the stress of looking after a sick child. I was able to reflect on the rough times I had been through, and gain a sense of purpose. Being happier definitely helped me to manage my gut problems and once again I was able to socialise and enjoy life.

I joined an orienteering club so I could start running to keep fit. This also gave me the opportunity to use my brain and body at the same time as it meant reading a map while trying to find controls in a forest. My mantra became "never knowingly last" as I joined in orienteering competitions around the UK and Europe and usually came in last but one!

I also joined a hash house harrier club. For those of you who don't know what hashing is, it's known as a drinking club with a running problem! We usually met at a pub where the leader (called a hare) would lay a trail through fields, roads and woodland with flour with false trails along the way to add to the confusion of finding the right way. At the end of the trail the hash would reach the pub at around the same time and socialise with a couple of drinks.

This definitely helped me to forget about all the issues I had lived through. I finally had a group of people with whom I could socialise and talk with, have fun and keep fit at the same time. Whenever I laid a hash I made sure that everyone went through a play park to go on the swings and slides. There's so much fun being out in the fresh air and playing in a play park!

It helped to keep my gut health in check and gave me a reason to keep going. However, I still didn't have the skills to understand how to manage my mental health when things went wrong.

I'm sure life events happen for a reason. They happen so that we can learn lessons from them to make ourselves stronger in the event of a disaster. My learnings were that I needed to find ways of developing more resilience in order to improve the way I managed my life.

Dealing With More Trauma

Roll on August 2013. We were travelling back from a holiday in Cornwall and planning to travel to London to see our eldest son as it was his birthday that day. However, after two hours of travelling the driver of the car on the opposite carriageway was not paying attention to what was ahead of him on the road. The cars in front of him were slowing down but he was oblivious to this until it was too late.

As he reached the car directly in front of him he had to swerve to avoid hitting the car. Instead of hitting the car in front of him he veered across the carriageway and smashed into our car.

He had been travelling at around 50mph and we had also been travelling at around the same speed coming towards him on the other side of the road. A sudden crashing noise startled me as I had not been paying attention to the traffic around us. A silence developed and a burning smell from the airbags filled the car. Suddenly pain hit me in my stomach where the seat belt had pressed against me during the crash. I was in agony. My daughter also started to cry out in pain. My husband was stunned and unable to communicate for a few minutes and my son who had been in the passenger seat had a cut to his hand but seemed to have survived without any major injuries.

We were rushed to hospital where my daughter was found to have internal bleeding and I had fractures to my back and ribs. My husband and son managed to avoid any major injuries but did have whiplash.

It took three months to recover from the injuries sustained in the crash and a further six months to gain full strength in my body. It had been devastating going through the trauma of the accident, but we had come out of it alive and all made a recovery. I became so much more grateful for each day after going through such a traumatic event.

It taught me to value each day so much more than I had done before. I became even more determined to look after my health, so I ventured into training to become a Life Coach and NLP Master Practitioner. I learnt so many skills to stay buoyant in times of strife, and how to understand the intricacies of the conscious and unconscious mind. I started to apply these newly learnt tools to my job in occupational health as well as to myself. It made such a difference to my life and to helping clients in the workplace. Having these tools meant that I could help other people to transform their lives in a way I had never been able to do before. It was so satisfying and rewarding to be able to help people in this way!

New Learnings After Another Hospital Admission

Although I now had the tools to success with my mindset and to make changes to improve my own resilience, I was still suffering from bouts of gut ache, bloating, indigestion and overall poor gut health. I hadn't realised how important diet was to maintain a healthy gut until I ended up in hospital with a massive gut infection.

I had been feeling slightly unwell for a few days until I could no longer eat or drink due to severe abdominal pain. I ended up in A&E in Bath and was assessed over several hours. Eventually I was sent to a ward and monitored by the nurses. Following a scan I was diagnosed with a massive gut infection. I had a drip and was given three different drugs to combat the infection making me feel extremely nauseous. I was not allowed to eat for four days and lay in bed in pain and feeling sorry for myself.

When I was discharged I was advised to have a soft diet for a few days and then build up my diet. That was the total sum of dietary advice I was given. Despite my nursing background I had no idea how to manage my diet or my gut issues to prevent another flare up. At that point I decided to study further with the Health Sciences Academy to become a gut health advisor.

Only after the training did I realise how important it is to eat the right foods to keep the body healthy. I learnt all about the microbiome and how it helps to prevent infection and inflammation. I also learnt about supplements including probiotics, Turmeric, Zinc, Vitamin D and Vitamin B complex amongst others.

I finally had a roadmap to keep my gut healthy through eating the correct foods. I no longer suffered from all the gut distress I had suffered from on and off for the last 30 years.

I now help women on how to manage their lifestyle to avoid gut distress and am loving every minute of it. It is so cathartic to see other women who have been grappling with gut distress to overcome their issues and come out the other side healthier and happier with the knowledge base to stay healthy for the long term.

I am grateful for all the training I have implemented as there is nothing more rewarding than passing on knowledge to other people to help them overcome significant issues in their life.

I just wish I had found the tools to cope with all the trauma in my life earlier. Learning to deal with emotional turmoil is one of the greatest gifts anyone can ask for, so when life gets tough always look for support from family or friends. Learn to meditate or learn other techniques to keep your brain from becoming your enemy.

About Me

I am a Gut Health Coach. I help menopausal women suffering from gut distress to change their diet and lifestyle so they can get on with their day feeling with more energy, confidence and concentration in their life allowing them to enjoy their renewed relationships with food, friends and family.

Against The Tide

Dr. Oma Peters
Pharmacist, Entrepreneur, Mentor
Mental Wellness Intelligence Network (MentalWIN)

"If my childhood memories are filled with the ringing taunt that "Girls can't be...," they are further filled with the more devastating cry that "Coloured females can't be... "
– Gloria Powell

Looking at the immaculately dressed female nurse on that sunny Monday afternoon left a permanent impression on my psyche. It was the days the nurses' uniform was a white dress and a white hair piece pinned to their hair. This nurse looked impeccable. I admired her show of empathy and kindness. I admired her for other reasons I could not place a finger on...The government of the African country where I grew up initiated a polio eradication program and immunisation centres were set up in rural areas across the country. Such a wide spread immunisation exercise was unusual in the little village and it took several meetings with the elders and a lot of sensitisation and persuasion for the community members to accept and engage with the program. As a girl born in the northern part of this African country, I found it fascinating seeing a few non-locals around but this nurse stood out…at least to me.

Life in this village was simple and it was fun growing up. The most fun part for me was having so many playmates around. The houses were without boundaries and everyone was more than just neighbours to one another. We looked out for one another and shared the little that there was. The fathers went out in groups early in the morning to the farms as subsistent agriculture was the main source of livelihood. Life was pretty simple.

However, the thought of having a western education was a far-fetched dream. The only school around at the time was a primary school and it was outside the village, a long trek away. Moreover, the female gender was not expected to amount to much. Her value was in house-keeping and child-bearing and she was to be seen (just) but not heard. Value was not placed on the girl child education and this was often opposed, after all, she was only going to grow up, have many kids and raise them. Girls got given away in marriage quite early and who the girls got married to was entirely the choice of the parents and older relations. This was the tradition. Although I had heard tales of women who were severely punished and then banished from the village for refusing their parent's choice of husband, no one known to me at the time ever went against it. From an early age, these tales were told to girls to deter them as they were warned of the repercussions. So, aspiring to be anything other than an under-aged wife and mother was unheard of.

New Goals, New Dreams

The nurse's professionalism was admirable. She spoke kindly to every child and reassured parents of the benefits of the immunisation. I liked her. I thought about her on the long walk home with my mother after I had received my immunisation and woke up the next day thinking to myself... 'I would like to be like this nurse and help people'.

That afternoon, I found myself walking to the immunisation centre alone, hoping the nurse was still there. 'If only I could catch a glimpse of her again', I thought to myself as I got closer to the centre. From a distance, I spotted her, in her immaculate white dress. My face beamed with a smile as my heart raced in excitement. I watched until a time she appeared to be less busy. I walked towards her, inched forward until I was close enough to be heard. At this time, I spoke only my native tongue and it was clear she was not a native. I still ventured to say hello in my native tongue. I was surprised when she responded. (I later learned that the medical team were taught a few common words and sentences in the native dialect, just enough to get by with the locals. No wonder, she said the same kind words to every child and the same words of reassurance to the mothers).

Her response made me feel welcome and this gave me a bit more confidence. I then said out loud, "I want to be like you, to wear the immaculate white dress you wear and help people". She did not understand this, so she turned to one of the locals who helped at the centre and spoke broken English, for interpretation. A smile broke out on her face afterwards.

She then told me through the interpreter that if I wanted to become like her, I would need to go to school and study hard.

That was all I needed. I hopped back home in excitement and announced to my parents that I would start going to school the next day. As expected, this was discouraged. I was lectured on the many reasons why going to school was the wrong path to tread. However, I was determined. My cousin's house was close to the only school outside the village which was more than a mile away. I used the excuse of meeting up with my cousin to leave the house. The school, owned and run by missionaries at the time was free, so I just turned up.

Embarking on a Fresh Journey

School was fun… until my parents discovered that I had been going to school. Following stern warnings, I was subjected to diverse forms of punishment to deter me from continuing. My teachers' (who believed I was doing well) plea to my parents made no difference. I was however determined to continue, so despite the discouragement and antagonism, I kept at it and excelled. By secondary school (high school), the missionaries gave scholarships to a few high performing students and I was one of them. I opted for one of their boarding schools which was located in a town about five hours drive from my village.

Needless to say, by this time, the antagonism was not just against me but against my family. Pressure mounted on my parents from relatives. My parents in turn mounted pressure on me -to desist from such! "No girl does this… the honour of a woman lies in marriage...and an early one", they said. All these seemed to strengthen my resolve to be educated and my determination grew with each passing day despite the struggle. Although there were times I wished I had the support of my family like the other kids, the encouragement from the teachers who understood my plight sufficed. I worked hard and it paid off. At the end of high school, I emerged the second-best graduating student of the year. This attracted a university scholarship award to study Pharmacy.

This was great news to me. I was inching further towards realising my dream of becoming a health professional, like the nurse I saw some years back. To my family back home, it was a slap in the face. I had kept their choice of husband for me waiting for this long and now I was off to university. It was nothing but shame and disgrace to the family. When they saw that their anger strengthened my resolve, my family changed tactics. They began to plead with me and this made me feel guilty and selfish. I considered giving up at this point. One night, I laid awake thinking about the choices before me. No one known to me with my background had towed this path before so, I had no one to speak to, no role model to look up to. I felt so alone in this battle. 'Suppose my parents were right...suppose things went horribly wrong in the university...' I thought to myself. But the more I weighed the options, the more convinced I became that going further to the university was the right thing to do. I had no idea what laid ahead but it felt right to further my education. I went ahead and accepted the offer.

University was again, a rough sail. I often wondered what I had got myself into. I would then conclude that since I was in it already, the only option I had was to succeed. Time appeared to pass quite quickly though, and soon it was the end of the program. Again, I successfully earned my degree. This news did not matter to my family but then, I was given another chance to accept another marriage offer (my parent's choice, of course). I was in my mid-twenties and now considered 'too old' for marriage. But then, my parents got a suitor who was happy to do them (and me) the 'favour' of marrying their 'very old' daughter…me.

For my family, turning down this 'opportunity' and insisting on marrying a boyfriend I met at Uni, was the height of insanity. All hell was let loose! Their fury was unimaginable. The anger and bitterness deepened, from family and extended relations alike. I was a disgrace! My parents were blamed for letting me, a girl, go to school. I became the black sheep of the family and no one wanted to have anything to do with me. Relatives warned their children to keep away from me.

Lost In The Shadows

I got a good job with one of the hospitals in a distant town and was excited. With my usual streak of hard work and dedication, I became more competent. I brought in a few innovative ideas that supported better pharmacological patient care and this impressed my boss. I was part of a friendly team and we spent time together outside work, socialising. So, life was good… or so I thought…until I realised that the long-standing trauma of rejection by my family had begun to take its toll on my mental health. Initially, I put it down to stress due to my desire to be a high performer at my place of work. I took a step back and delegated some roles as appropriate but my mental health suffered a further downward spiral as the months went by. I knew I was breaking down. The high levels of anxiety and other symptoms meant a whole lot of time off work. I so desperately wanted to be accepted by my family. I discussed these issues many times with my mentor, my university professor who took special interest in my welfare. He spurred me on to pursue my dreams, but the idea of leaving my boyfriend and going back home to accept my parent's marriage proposal played on my mind.

With diverse forms of therapies, I battled the issues with my mental health and I plodded on. There were good days and there were bad days. Eventually, I took the bold step and got married to my boyfriend, with no family in attendance although I reached out to them with gifts, desperate for their understanding and acceptance, all to no avail.

Shortly after my wedding, I was opportune to migrate to the United Kingdom with my husband. As you would imagine, adapting to the new environment and the whole new system took a lot of effort. Forming a new social network and preparing for my professional exams while working to pay the bills was quite demanding. I knew I had no choice but to get on with it. I was determined to succeed and even more determined to prove to my family that I had towed the right path all along. I wanted them to see a benefit in my 'rebellion'. And beyond my family, my dream to help people, just like the immaculately dressed nurse I had encountered many years back, remained alive.

Rising Amidst The Fall

A few weeks before I was due to sit my professional exams, it had snowed heavily and days later there were patches of black ice along the kerb. On my way to the nearby corner shop, never having experienced snow before then and so wearing the wrong shoes for the weather, I stepped on a patch of ice, slipped, fell and fractured my leg (around my shin) in two places. Conveyed in an ambulance, I spent some time in hospital after the operation to fix it. Following the operation, complications arose and this meant frequent hospital visits to different health professionals after my discharge from the hospital.

Soon, it was exam day and I hopped on crutches into the exam hall. Two weeks on, the results were out… and sadly, I failed. I cried so much and could hardly be consoled. Fortunately, there was an opportunity to re-sit the exam in a couple of months. However, I still struggled to prepare for the exams as my physical health still needed further attention. I gradually became discouraged and found it quite hard to cope. As time drew near, I reminded myself of the storms I had weathered through right from a very young age and how resilient I had been. I reminded myself of my dreams, my ambitions and this gave me a renewed hope. I told myself I could do it. I drew on this innate strength and decided to give the exam my best shot despite the odds. I picked up from there and studied hard.

Soon it was the day of the re-sit exam. On the train to the venue, I boosted my confidence with affirmations. I sat the exam and two weeks later, the results were out. This time, I passed! The feeling I had was a mix of relief and joy. Following on from this, my physical trauma healed quicker. I gave more attention to therapies that helped my mental health recovery. Recovery was fast and life generally improved. We (my husband and I) went on to build a family, having two lovely children- a boy and a girl.

No Looking Back

At this point, I teamed up with charity organisations to support women and children in rural areas. The difference this made to their lives was heartwarming. My ambition to impact lives and contribute to helping people live out their full potentials gave me the boost to aspire and achieve more. I believed I required more knowledge and skills to make this contribution effectively, so I went further to acquire a Master's degree. And with a desire to niche down on helping people in the area of mental health, having struggled in this area myself, I further pursued and acquired a PhD in Psychological therapies and mental health.

In addition, I invested in training and mentorship programmes. These were in the areas of business management and investments, leadership, self-development, interpersonal skills, networking, money mindset, public speaking and many more. I attended several conferences in and outside of Europe in my quest for more knowledge and I loved the transformation that came with these efforts. Following on, aside from my usual nine to five, I set up a pharmacy business. With the portfolios of trainings, qualifications and certifications I had acquired, I developed a framework that combined psychological models and business strategies. It's designed to improve profits, scale and grow a business without the need to spend more money or time on the business. Using this framework, my business grew and I expanded into property investments.

Looking to impact a wider audience, I founded the Mental Wellness Intelligence Network (MentalWIN). Bringing together my wealth of experience, the many trainings, the transformations, my academic qualifications, achievements and expertise, MentalWIN is designed to help business owners improve their profits, grow and scale their businesses without the need for more financial expenses. With MentalWIN, I work with companies, organisations, institutions and industries organising mental health first aid training with possible psychological therapies for the staff. I therefore contribute to improving the productivity and performance of their staff through this means which in turn improves their profit.

Since founding MentalWIN, one of my wins is having had the privilege of speaking at mental health conferences in Africa, Europe and Asia. In addition, I founded the Wealthy Woman Co. Here, I combine the wealth of my life's experience and my psychological therapy/mental health qualification to mentor women into a life of achievements while creating their independence through wealth building. But the rather emotional win for me was my family! My conscious effort such as sending emissaries with gifts to placate them, won them over at last! And I am happy this happened before my mum sadly passed. I attended her funeral and visited home a few times afterwards. In turn, my Dad visited me in the UK. He was only a young boy when the (then) queen visited my country of birth many years back, so my Dad was quite delighted to see the palace and witness the Changing of the Guard.

While there are more dreams to fulfil, it fills my heart with great joy that I did not give up. In the words of Laura Morgan Roberts, the answer to the question of what it takes to succeed can be reduced to a single capacity- resilience.

About Me

Oma Peters is an award-winning pharmacist and entrepreneur. With over 20 years experience as a pharmacist, Oma who holds a PhD in Psychological Therapies and Mental health has distinguished herself in the area of Mental Health. Today, Oma is the CEO of the Mental Wellness Intelligence Network (MentalWIN) UK as well as a director in other allied health companies. She trains business owners, company directors, work-place leaders, managers and supervisors on how to employ mental wellness strategies to improve the profit of their businesses

Conclusion

In the mix of these stories, resilience stands out as the common thread that binds them all together. Resilience goes beyond merely weathering the storm; it involves drawing valuable lessons from adversity, tragedy, loss, heartbreak, failure, or change, and shaping a purposeful path forward.

As you navigate your journey, be open to its unique twists, and at every turn, allow these powerful lessons offer you the wisdom needed to persistently forge ahead.

- Resilience is a skill - the more you stay committed to your goals, the stronger you become in handling unexpected challenges.
- Resilience is embracing your new reality and finding the strength to adapt with a positive outlook.
- Resilience is acknowledging that the power and responsibility to uplift yourself lie entirely within your own hands.
- Resilience involves extending kindness to yourself, particularly when navigating uncharted territory.

- Resilience is necessary to be able to unlock untapped potential.
- Resilience only blossoms when we cultivate the belief that the world holds significant opportunities waiting for us.

Challenges will always make themselves known, giving you the choice to either let setbacks define you or be shaped by the countless times you stood up and kept moving forward.

The motivation to keep moving forward has to start from you, and only then will you realise your success story is far greater than you ever thought possible.

About Queens In Business

Our Why

Today female entrepreneurs are making waves in the world of business. There have never been more of us rising up, standing up for what we believe in and building our own vehicle for freedom.

It's our belief that each and every female entrepreneur has what it takes to be successful. Everyone has a gift inside of them, a skill or knowledge that could help someone who is struggling right now.

Female entrepreneurs have the ability to contribute to the world and deserve the opportunity to be successful, feel fulfilled and be visible within their business.

But the journey of entrepreneurship can be challenging at times and with just a fraction of women taking the leap to start their own businesses it can be a lonely ride. That's why we created Queens In Business.

Queens In Business is more than just a community. It's a movement created to recognise the achievements of female entrepreneurs, to support and guide them and give them the tools to increase their exposure in business.

Co-founded by four of us, it's the first of its kind, created by female entrepreneurs for female entrepreneurs:

Chloë Bisson – The Authority Queen
Shim Ravalia – The Collaboration Queen
Sunna Coleman – The Writing Queen
Tanya Grant – The Branding Queen

Before starting QIB, we'd all built our own successful businesses, spent huge amounts of money on training and mentorship and invested years in growing our businesses.

We learned and mastered specific strategies and methods to get our businesses where they are today and we are now sharing those learnings and experiences with our clients.

Whether it is having a successful business or becoming financially independent, we aim to provide female entrepreneurs with the tools they need and a community to support them along the way.

Our Methodology

We believe that in business the ability to achieve success comes down to three core pillars:

- Education
- Empowerment
- Execution

Education for us means having the right skills, knowledge and strategies to achieve your goals and if you don't have them right now, having access to learn from experts that do.

Empowerment is about surrounding yourself with the right people to support you and cheer for you on the journey. It is about creating an empowering environment that nourishes you to be the best that you can be.

Execution means having the motivation, determination and drive to do what it takes to get to your end goal. Where we may struggle to find the motivation within ourselves, it's about having mentors to encourage you and giving you a kick up the bum when you need it.

At Queens In Business, we've created a powerful methodology that combines all three of the core pillars. We provide the hands-on business education from world class experts with the push you need to execute your strategies whilst surrounding you with supportive members to empower you to overcome any roadblocks that come up on the way.

Our Mission

We're on a mission to change the world of entrepreneurship. We want to create a movement that empowers female entrepreneurship and encourages their drive for success, not belittles it or judges them for putting their career first.

We want to eliminate the fear of judgement and the fear of failure. We want to create a world where it's okay to ask for help, it's okay to express your challenges and it's okay to make mistakes.

We want to support female entrepreneurs in becoming powerful role models for future generations who will believe in their abilities and believe they can achieve what they want.

It's our mission to provide support and exposure to Queens all over the world regardless of their age, background, or their position in their business.

It's time now for female entrepreneurs to rise up and be leaders, fight for what they want for themselves and for others, and get seen with confidence.

To find out more about Queens In Business, go to:
www.queensinbusinessclub.com

Contact us on:
team@queensinbusinessclub.com

Printed in Great Britain
by Amazon

39893124R00139